Praise for *Comedy FAQs and Answers*

"No one has written a more comprehensive and interesting and illuminating book on the subject of stand-up comedy than our Dave Schwensen."—Budd Friedman, Founder of Improv Comedy Clubs

"Dave's book speaks from the heart. He's been there, he's done that. And now he's giving the information for others who want to become one. This book is definitely worthwhile to read and to follow."—Roger Paul, Comedy Agent, ICM

"Dave truly understands the reality of today's stand-up business. This should be required reading for anyone considering a career in comedy."—Kurtis Matthews, Owner, San Francisco Comedy College

COMEDY FAQs AND ANSWERS

HOW THE STAND-UP BIZ *REALLY* WORKS

Dave Schwensen

ALLWORTH PRESS
NEW YORK

DEDICATION

In memory of Edward Schwensen and Carrol Harrison: Your laughter is missed, but always remembered.

Dedicated to those of you who love to laugh, and are inspired to bring that joy to others.

To Debbie, Kevin, Arlys, Blake, and Brooke.

To my son Paul who was first entrusted with the secret that I was writing this book—and didn't tell anyone! Now, if I just could get him to be as tight-lipped about my age, my weight . . . You're the inspiration for my laughter.

08 07 06 05 04   5 4 3 2 1

Published by Allworth Press
An imprint of Allworth Communications, Inc.
10 East 23rd Street, New York, NY 10010

Cover design by Derek Bacchus
Interior design by Sharp Designs, Inc., Lansing, MI
Page composition/typography by Integra Software Services, Pvt. Ltd., Pondicherry, India
ISBN: 1-58115-411-9

Library of Congress Cataloging-in-Publication Data

Schwensen, Dave.
    Comedy FAQs and answers: how the stand-up biz really works/Dave
    Schwensen.
      p. cm.
    Includes index.
    ISBN 1-58115-411-9 (pbk.)
    1. Stand-up comedy—Vocational guidance.   I. Title.

PN1969.C65S37 2005
792.702'8'023—dc22

2004029553

Printed in Canada

CONTENTS

1 PRE-STAGE

② ON STAGE

③ OFF STAGE

④ BACKSTAGE

THANK YOU

This book would not have been possible without the help of friends and business associates. The following list includes both. Many were an integral part of actually putting this together, while others were simply valuable influences. All deserve mention and my sincerest thank you:

Budd Friedman and Fran Cowan at The Improv; my agent Joan Brandt; Alison Leslie and Melanie Herschorn at Maleah Leslie & Associates; Yvette Shearer at Shearer Public Relations; Rory Rosgarten; Jonathan Mooves, Joe Khoury, and Loan T. Dang; Bill Bowley and Charles Montgomery from Power Entertainment; Susan Phillips and Jerry Hamza from Carlin Productions; Maggie Houlehan at Parallel Entertainment; Kate Madigan; Mike Berkowitz and Pamela King at Rick Dorfman Entertainment; Tony Ross at Personal Publicity; Christopher Pratt and Brie at A Management Company; Roger Paul at ICM; Mario Gonzalez, Frank Kondrich, Lee Herlands, Sarah Nye, John Count, and Dave Carpenter at The Improv; Nick Kostis and John Lorince at Hilarities; June Moes, Steve Hofstetter, Lord Carrett, and Mike Sergio, (who now owes me big time for this mention).

My teammates on the legendary NYC Ironmen Softball Team for leading the league in laughs: Fat Mikey, Frankie G., Mio, Carter, Billy Action, JoMama, Conrad, Murphy; team owners, Bob and Marlene; team cocktail waitresses, Sally, Cindy, and Vicky; chief of team insecurity, Led Lacy; and Brian Doyle Murray, for color commentary and getting me on *Saturday Night Live*.

The Brothers of Delta Tau Delta Fraternity at Bowling Green State University in Ohio for inspiration about "hecklers," including Chuck Sprosty who would embarrass me in front of large groups of people if I didn't mention his name.

John, Paul, George, and Ringo. Groucho, Harpo, Chico, and Zeppo. Mick and Keith. Moe, Larry, Curly, and Shemp. Dean and Jerry. Tom and Dick.

All past and future members of my comedy workshops. I learned as much from you as you did from me.

PREFACE

Let's get started. . . .

The houselights go down. Except for candles on each table flickering like stars in the night, the showroom itself is dark. Audience members turn their attention toward the stage where a lone microphone stands illuminated in bright spotlight.

A voice over the sound system welcomes everyone to the club and promises a laugh-filled evening. The first comedian is announced, the crowd applauds, you start walking toward the stage—and you abruptly stop.

"Wait a minute!" You might say, interrupting the scene I'm trying to set in your mind. "What am I supposed to do?"

"What do you want to do?" I'd say.

"Make people laugh," you'd continue. "That's what comedians do, right?"

"Yeah, last time I checked. Just do that."

"What would I say? Something funny?"

"That's a good start," I'd agree. "Try that."

Easy to do? For some it can be. For others, performing comedy takes hard work, dedication, and experience. The common ingredient is talent. The goal is to make audiences laugh. When it all comes together, a good comedian can make it look easy.

This book is the result of hard work, dedication, and experience. The common ingredient is worthwhile advice. The goal is to shine a bright spotlight on your path into the comedy world and make the journey toward success a bit easier than it would be without advice.

But writing this book wasn't all work and no play. I laughed a lot writing it—it was impossible not to when talking with so many talented, funny, and successful comedians. The main ingredient of this business is humor, and you'll find a generous portion within these pages.

All the contributors have one thing in common: I happen to be a big fan of each and every one. Otherwise, they wouldn't be included. Many are friends I've known since the beginning of my career as Talent Coordinator for The Improv Comedy Clubs in both New York and Los Angeles, and for the television show *A&E's An Evening At The Improv*. Others are comedians I've booked through my agency (Dave Schwensen Entertainment), for corporate events, college shows, or nightclubs, interviewed for my newspaper columns, or searched out specifically for advice on certain topics. Some are stars, while others may not be household names—yet—but "insiders" know who they are.

I've also worked at various points in my career with all the behind-the-scenes members of this illustrious group. Each is a true professional with valuable experience and advice. Plus, they're as entertaining as some comedians—and I didn't have to pay a cover charge for the laughs! To say their advice about the inner workings of the comedy industry is worthwhile is an understatement.

So, let's get started—again. . . .

"Is it really that easy?" You may ask, as the audience grows impatient waiting for you to take the stage.

"If it was easy, then more people would be comedians," I'd reply. "But if you work hard, dedicate yourself, and get experience . . ."

"I know! I know! You said that already!"

". . . then it's worth the effort. If you want it bad enough."

"I do," you'd answer, moving toward the stage.

"That's a good start," I'd say to myself, before grabbing an empty seat in the back of the showroom for a laugh-filled evening.

Keep laughing!!

—DAVE SCHWENSEN

Note: Credits for all of my contributors are listed in the back of the book. All contributors are stand-up comedians, except where otherwise identified.

INTRODUCTION

To be a successful comedian, you have to be funny. That's the bottom line and the number one goal; to make audiences laugh. Except it's not always as easy as the good comics make it look. There are many other factors that play a huge part in achieving success in the business; by "success" I mean being hired on a regular basis to perform comedy.

Creativity, being unique, and having an original point of view are talents that need to be explored, sharpened, and used to develop comedy material and an individual presence. It's also important to have on-stage experience at verbalizing these thoughts, observations, or jokes, along with a willingness to reveal and explore your personality in front of a room full of strangers.

In the world of comedy, these factors are accomplished in two ways: performing and writing. Creating comedy is comparable to making music, painting a picture, or writing a book. In other words, comedy is an art and the creators are artists.

Once you're committed to doing comedy (rather than committed *for* doing comedy), all these above factors will come into play. You can also bet you'll encounter a few more along your journey, especially since achieving success in any business usually includes having an understanding of the business methods.

As a performer and writer, your best teacher will be experience. An audience will always tell you what's funny—and what's not. You'll learn to make adjustments, restructure your material and delivery, and then climb back on stage to go through the whole process again and again. Talent and determination are the foundation in becoming a successful comedian.

Then again, a little luck never hurts. Being in the right place at the right time is an underlying theme in many success stories. This is the "unknown factor" you can't always control, but it's possible to put the odds in your favor. The best way is to be seen by people who can further your career. And the best way to let them know you should be seen is through funny performances and good promotion.

This book will answer your questions about these topics. In fact, that's the main purpose, answering questions. How do you start? How do you write? Where do you perform? What can you do to make your performances better? How can you be seen by people who can put the odds in your favor of becoming a successful comedian?

Thanks to a background in the comedy industry and a knack for self-promotion, I've received quite a few letters and e-mails—from around the world—from hopeful and professional comedians asking for more details about these subjects and many others. In my comedy workshops, I've given out "homework" (here, that term means the opposite of what it did during our school days). In this case, I asked aspiring comics to write down their questions about the industry, and I did the work of answering them.

Along the way, I've had the opportunity to talk and work with some of the top comedians, agents, producers, publicists, coaches, club owners, and talent bookers in the business. Since I'll never claim to "know it all," I've relied on their experiences, thoughts, opinions, and advice about the industry for more insight into the topics. These are people I truly respect and admire.

Putting all the pieces together, the final result is that this book includes questions from people not only thinking about getting into the business, but also many who are working and making a living at their chosen career. The answers come from experience.

An avowed pack rat, I've saved all this correspondence. That's probably why I'll never fit into the corporate world, because I'd be the suspect leaving a long paper trail for anyone to investigate. Except in this case, there's nothing to hide. It's information from the comedy trenches and if it saves time during your personal investigation into the comedy world, then filling up notebooks, tape recorders, and my computer hard drive has been well worth the effort.

These questions and answers have been divided into four sections devoted to the various phases of developing a successful career in comedy: Pre-Stage, On Stage, Off Stage, and Backstage. We'll cover the craft of being an artist and the methods behind the business for those of you who want to make the commitment sooner, rather than later. You'll also hear from many comics and industry professionals who have "been there and done that."

To give you an idea of what I'm rambling about, here's an example of a thought that undoubtedly runs through everyone's mind early in his or her stand-up career. 'Do I really have a chance at being successful?' Well, it all depends. . . .

FAQ **What Are My Chances?**

Greetings Dave,

Thanks so much for taking time to really watch my videotape. I have a question. This is a big one and I hesitate to ask, but do you think I have the potential to "make it?" I know there are a million variables to making it in the entertainment business and how we can all be the best if we just apply ourselves. But do you see real talent in my act? —T.D.

I'm the wrong person to ask if you can "really make it." Do you want to know why? Because I've worked with *too* many comedians who were told early in their careers that they would *never* make it. You just don't know and can't truly make that decision without really digging in and doing it for at least a few years. I don't know how long you've been performing comedy, but if you can still remember the exact number of shows you've done, I'll dare to say it's not long enough to really hit your potential as a performer and writer.

I was asked this same question during one of my recent workshops. We'd only just had our first meeting in which everyone did a short comedy set, when I received a call the next day from a young woman wanting to know if I thought she had the potential to be a comedian. She was going to base her whole decision about pursuing comedy on what she had done in a workshop on the first day—without taking time to develop her act and get experience in front of an audience. How could I, or anyone else for that matter, possibly know what direction her material would eventually take or how her performances will develop as she gains experience on stage?

Only the performer can make that personal decision and it can only be made after he's tested the waters and developed his talent as far as he thinks possible. If there comes a point where the performances are not working and the comic has exhausted his creative and on-stage talents without success, then it's probably time to start thinking about doing something else. But if comedy is in his blood and it's a passion he can't imagine replacing with anything else, there really is no choice in the matter. He keeps climbing on stage and looking for a spotlight of hope—which is also known as the light at the end of the tunnel.

Great comics do it because they *have* to and sometimes success comes from that passion. Other comics have different reasons, including the desire to be rich and famous. These can also be powerful incentives, but those performers probably have a better chance of achieving their goals by working hard at their craft instead of daydreaming about dollar signs and television deals.

You need to make a decision. Are you willing to work hard, sacrifice, and dedicate yourself to this career? Do you want it bad enough that this is not even a decision at all? If so, then the question about "making it" will be answered in its own due time—by you.

Richard Jeni

Everybody sucks in the beginning. I mean, it took about two years to become . . . effective. You know? I don't mean good, I mean effective. To the point where you can be reasonably sure the audience wouldn't totally hate you. It took about five years to get pretty good. And that's only pretty good. It's really hard. I've never seen anybody that's really that good in comedy who hasn't been doing it at least five years. It takes a really long time. You have to learn how to write material as well as perform it. You have to really get both of those things down.

Part One PRE-STAGE

1 PRE-STAGE

FAQ 1 *Am I* a **Comedian?**

I was down at the library a couple years ago and a book about comedy reached out and smacked me right in the face. That's when the idea of stand-up first occurred to me. I know you don't know me, but right now I am going through a lot in my life. After years of working at a factory, the company shut it down. I'm on the verge of losing my house and everything I own. My mother is old and can't remember hardly anything and I'm the only one to take care of her. I believe if it wasn't for stand-up in my life right now, I would go insane. —D.L.

You've made a very profound statement not only about what's going on in your life, but also offered deep insight into why many creative and driven individuals have a need to perform stand-up comedy. For some, it's not a choice. It could be as complicated as self-therapy, or a way to relieve stress that doesn't involve lawyer fees, court dates, or an alibi. For others, stand-up comedy is purely a way of expressing themselves and being heard. Of course, we can't discount the excitement of making people laugh or the high that comes from performing and being in the spotlight.

There's no one reason that's right for everyone. They all work, it just depends on which ones work for you.

Being successful at comedy is not easy. If it was, everyone would do it for any of the above reasons and others I haven't even mentioned. Then again, life in general is hardly easy, as you've pointed out. Sometimes just looking forward to a laugh—given or received—is enough to keep pushing us into this crazy business.

It's difficult when you're starting out in comedy. You either know this already or will soon find out. The comics who continue to follow their career path and learn something every step along the way have the best chance of making their dreams of success come true.

Wait a minute, did I just say "chance?" Possibly the wrong word. . . .

Yes, chance and luck often come into play, but the comics who have experience, knowledge of the business, dedication, and drive can steer themselves into a position to make things happen. Where it all leads, no one can predict. But then again, no one ever finds out unless they try.

You have a lot of factors that could prevent you from becoming a comedian. Throw in an ex-wife, a dog, and a pick-up truck, and you could be a country music superstar. But obviously, that's not where your heart is.

Everyone going into comedy can find reasons why they shouldn't. If you can't think of reasons yourself, then I suggest mentioning this topic during a conversation with your parents, teachers, spouses, employers, co-workers, friends, or just about anyone else who might not share the same dream. Believe me, you'll discover there are no shortages of reasons that can work against you.

Except the bottom line is no one can make that choice for you. Especially in the beginning of your journey, because you'll probably have to make that same decision everyday:

'Am I a comedian or not?'

Are you? I don't know. You don't know either, unless you try. There are many personal and business factors you'll have to think about seriously, along with unforeseen problems that will need to be solved. If you're not sure comedy is your destined career, then have a backup plan. If there's no choice in the matter and you're driven to succeed, then reduce the element of chance and work hard toward gaining enough experience and knowledge to put yourself in a position to make things happen.

By the way, I'm very pleased a book on comedy jumped off the bookshelf and struck you in the face. The one you're currently reading is meant to hit you with the intensity of a sucker punch that will knock you into the next phase of your no-choice career: comedy.

Here's A Start

- **Job Requirements.** From the moment you decide to be a comedian, you take on a number of different jobs. You're a performer, director, manager, agent, and publicist. Except there wouldn't be work for any of these positions unless you first become a writer. This job has one requirement: create material that makes audiences laugh. How do you do that? Making it funny is a good idea. . . .

- **Say Something Funny.** Anyone can talk about any subject and bore people to tears, but a great comedian can talk about anything and make people laugh. Find what's humorous about what you want to say—real or imagined—and use it when writing your comedy material. Remember, if you say something and make it funny, you're a comedian. If you say something and it's not funny, you're not yet a comedian. If you're not sure where you fit in, you might want to think about hosting a game show or going into politics (which are not that much different from each other anyway). But here's something to consider—why did you think it was funny enough to say on a comedy stage in the first place? Understand why, learn how to convey it to an audience—and *that's* saying something funny.

- **Open Mike.** Yeah, you'll find out about this real quick. . . . Basically, any club that will let a performer with little or no experience get on stage to entertain an audience.

Margaret Cho

I was an opening act for, like, eight years. Then I middled for two weeks and then I was a headliner. So I never really got to enjoy the idea of just working as a comic because it was a struggle, then it was kind of fun for a while, and then it was another struggle. So, I've always had a hard time, I think.

And I was desperate to make a living. I did every job imaginable just to stay devoted. I kept getting fired because I'd get comedy gigs and do those instead of a regular job. So I understand that striving. I think if anything, that just makes you funnier because it makes you really needing and wanting it more and trying it more.

Understand that you don't do comedy as a hobby. You do it because you have to. You do it because there's nothing else in your life that you'd rather do. It's a strange compulsion and it's an obsession. It's an addiction. You just have to. And I think it's an insult for comedy for someone to come in and say, 'Oh, I just want to do comedy part-time.' I mean it's okay to come in and see if you want to do it, or whatever. If you're curious about it. But to be a stand-up comic, it takes everything.

FAQ 2 What Material Should I Use?

I'm just starting comedy and pondering my last two performances. I wanted to ask you about material. I don't write jokes. I go on stage and talk about whatever's on my mind. I've always been like that and have always been able to make it funny.

I did a set two weeks ago and everybody laughed. My next set, nobody laughed. To me, that's a red flag that it wasn't working. Should I just stick to doing the same material (that worked), over and over? I'm afraid I'll get bored, which is why I enjoy the concept of doing different sets based on whatever's on my mind at that moment. I'm starting to feel like I want to scrap everything (especially after this last show), and just try something else—perhaps actually writing a joke (what a concept!). Any opinions? —M.C.

I made a pot of coffee this morning. This is not something I do every day, but enough that I don't find it a very exciting activity. If I haven't had enough sleep (one incentive to drink coffee), or I'm distracted (like the time our dog made a meal out of my television remote control), I might make a mistake and add the wrong amount of coffee or water.

Sometimes I'll get lucky and enjoy a new caffeine experience. Other times I'll have to pour the concoction down the sink and try to salvage what's left of the morning by making another pot with my usual amounts to get a better taste.

Making coffee—uh, excuse me—making comedy . . . is a matter of taste. Sometimes it's good to know what ingredients on which you can depend to get the desired results. Then again, trying something new is never boring and if you're lucky, you could enjoy a new comedy experience.

Doing the same routine night after night can be boring—if you let it. Making up a completely new act every performance could be enough of a comedy jolt to make caffeine obsolete; unless it's going down the drain and taking you with it. The perfect mix might be a little of each, but it all depends on your personal taste.

Some comics enjoy familiarity. Others enjoy living dangerously. You can pick one or the other—or a combination of both. It's your choice.

Whatever you decide, whether it's writing material to use for every show or creating it on stage, one of the keys to success is picking topics that are most interesting to *you*. It could be insane one-line gags or characters that show-off your warped sense of humor, lengthy monologues about your life or something in the news that caught your attention. If you're working off the audience, someone's shirt might catch your eye or what they're drinking, whom they're sitting with, or even why they're laughing so hard (or why they're not!).

Your performance will have much more of an impact on an audience if *you* are interested in what you are saying. If you're writing material only because you think the audience will like it, but you don't particularly find it interesting, it won't work as well. I see this in my comedy workshops quite often. A comedian will get on stage and talk about something that is essentially meaningless to her. But within the set she'll hit on a subject *she* is really interested in and you can see the difference in her eyes, facial expressions, gestures, and delivery. I call this the "coming alive" moment and the goal is to have the entire performance "alive."

In other words, the topics really don't matter to an audience as long as they're laughing. But comedians need to pick ones they think are funny and personally interesting. If the performer buys into it, there's a good chance the audience will too.

It takes talent to write good comedy material. It also takes talent to walk on stage and improvise a new act every night. Which is the right choice for you? I won't even make a guess because only your personal experience can answer that question. Of course I do have an opinion since I find the topic interesting. . . .

Don't be fooled into thinking your favorite late-night television host writes a new monologue for every show. That's why staff writers earn a weekly paycheck. If you have proven material that gets laughter from an audience, don't hesitate to use it again and again; especially if your paycheck depends on that result. Chances are good your audience will be different for every show. They will never have heard your material before, so remember why you thought it was interesting and funny in the first place—then share it with them for the first time.

If you're improvising and the audience is laughing, you're a success. If you can do it at every show, you're also very talented. But if you're distracted for any reason (when's the last time you saw your dog *and* the remote control?), you'll have to rely on your talent to get you through, or have proven material ready to salvage the set. I've heard many of the best improvisers use the same descriptive term for audience members at different shows. When they've needed it, it was there for them.

Now the choice is up to you. The beauty is that you can change your mind every day. If it's the wrong mix, dump it down the sink and brew up another one.

Charles Fleischer

I used to do an act—kind of like everybody, although it wasn't like everybody because it was my own version of everybody. And before I went into my material, I would kind of work the crowd a little bit. Then one night, I think it was in Indianapolis, I realized that I had the light to get off and I hadn't gotten to any material yet. And then it was just a slow process of developing that into a structure that I use now. It took years, of course, to develop to what it is.

I think I've always found it to be the most exciting way to work. I mean I still . . . Like when I recorded my CD, for instance, that was an A to Z set. You know, worked on and crafted so the bits blended into each other and that's fun doing that as well. But there's something about going out and doing real-time stuff that creates a dangerous attitude that is picked up by the audience. And they realize that there's a danger to it and it just makes things a little more exciting. Because they know it's happening in real-time.

FAQ 3 Do I Gotta Write What They Wanna Hear?

When writing comedy material, I planned to focus on just the things I want to talk about. But in the last few days, I've actually been trying to write stuff that I didn't really want to do. Mainly it was things that I felt obligated to do from outside influences who keep telling me what I should or shouldn't put in my act. I find myself just wanting to say, 'Hey! Who's on stage? ME!' I'm sure they all mean well. —J.S.

There are two ways to look at this situation. Taking on the role of an optimist, I'm assuming you've impressed everyone with your talent and they now think of you as a comedian. Suggestions are meant to further your career, similar to successful comics who are "pitched" jokes by comedy writers.

On the other hand, if you wanted to play pessimist . . . Try to keep a positive attitude: These "others" are not suggesting you get out of the business! Obviously, their motive is meant to keep you going.

Almost everyone will have an opinion about what you do on stage, and it's important not to shut yourself off from that. If you're not getting laughs from an audience, then other opinions should be considered that could lead to changes made in your act. If they are laughing, your "collaborators" are showing a supportive opinion about what you're doing.

We'll talk later on about comics "writing" while on stage, but it's a method where the comic uses audience suggestions and opinions about certain topics to influence the direction of his act. The general idea is to continue working with whatever it is that gets laughs and mold it into a finished piece of performance material. Of course, the comic must also have his own thoughts and opinions about what is being said. After all, he will make the final decision on whether it becomes part of the act or discarded.

The bottom line is having something *you* want to say with your own personal sense of humor and delivery—even if the idea comes from someone else. It's true you're the one on stage and will ultimately have to answer to the audience reaction. But that's what good comedians do, including those who employ writers—they're still performing material that personally works for them.

Admittedly, even an optimist wouldn't say I've written anything resembling a comedy routine with this answer. But the message should be clear because I'm saying what I *want* to say—even though you gave me the original thought.

Ray Romano

I talk about my life. I don't do topical or political material. I talk about whatever happens. I talk about the kids. What you see in my (live) show is basically me, but it's stand-up so it's a little more uncensored. But you know me, I'm pretty clean. I talk about what any married guy would talk about. And if it's sex, it's the lack of it. That's all it is.

A lot of people who come to the live shows know me as the guy on the sitcom. Some of them don't even know that I do stand-up. They start to think . . . 'Wow!'

I didn't realize that until I did a gig in Mississippi. When you're in Los Angeles, nobody pays attention no matter who you are. When I went to Mississippi, then I realized, 'God, people think . . . Hey, we're fooling people! They think I'm somebody!' In Mississippi, it's either me, or the clay-shooting champion.

FAQ 4 Would a Comedy Class Help Me Put Together My Act?

I would like a little more insight on putting together a comedy act. I don't have any kind of set prepared, so I've thought about taking a comedy class. If I decide to do this, would I need to have a routine ready or would a comedy class be a bare-bones activity? —A.G.

Many comedy clubs and performing arts schools offer comedy workshops on a regular basis that fit the "bare bones" description—even when it's not Halloween. (Sorry, but I couldn't help "boning" up on a little humor myself.) A good way to find out where and when workshops are offered is to call clubs in your area, look in the entertainment sections of local newspapers, or search the Internet under "comedy" or "stand-up comedy."

The term "comedy class" is often used, but for someone with a creative mind (a valuable asset in the laughter biz), the image could stir up memories of a formal education where instructors taught proven facts. You know the drill: listen to the teacher, learn the exact formulas, and you'll pass. For students who like to color outside the lines, these scholastic restrictions might have actually taught them to start looking at comedy as a viable career option.

It's difficult to believe anyone can actually "teach" comedy, because it's a personal and artistic expression based on talent and developed through experience in front of an audience. There is no proven formula for writing a joke if you want to be creative, unique, and successful in this business. You'd have more luck trick-or-treating for jokes on Halloween than following someone else's technique on a comedy stage; unless you don't mind going to the party wearing the same costume as the funny guy who arrived earlier and got all the candy.

There are no guaranteed outlines for writing jokes, even though there are plenty of books and comedy teachers who claim to have the secret formula.

A successful comic may have his own technique or "hook" to rely on when writing material, but the reason it works for him and not for everyone else is because he's an individual. There's no one else who looks at, thinks about, or talks about everything *exactly* the same way he does.

You, as a comedian, are as unique as anyone else. And to stand out in stand-up, you must develop your own comedy voice.

Even the best writers and performers can't always predict how an audience will respond to untried or formulated material. Comedy acts, television and movie scripts, comic skits, and improvisational games can be written, borrowed, rewritten, rehearsed, and filmed before being presented, but production companies, investors, and performers can tell you they never know for sure if it works until the audience starts laughing. If you need more proof, keep track of all the sitcoms premiered each television season that have "proven" stars, writers, or producers. At the end of the year, how many are still on the air? With the huge amounts of money that can be made or lost, you can bet the creative minds behind each show made their best effort to predict what an audience would laugh at. But even these experts can be wrong, which is why the television graveyard is littered with canceled sitcoms.

The term "comedy workshop" carries a different meaning, which also serves as a guideline in what to look for if you decide not to enter the comedy world alone. These types of sessions should be productive meetings with a variety of people developing their individual comedy ideas and styles, while also offering helpful insight to others. Comedy can't be taught, but it can be influenced, brought out, and guided in a way that gives performers focus and direction. A new comedian might only need assurance that what he's writing is already funny. Other times an outside opinion can find humor in material the performer wasn't aware of or ever considered presenting on a comedy stage.

Similar to performing live in a comedy club, the audience reaction in a workshop is instantaneous. But along with the laughs (or dreaded silence), you get positive feedback and, if you didn't get any laughs, you'll get educated guesses as to why you didn't. In this setting, it's important the suggestions are also constructive and geared toward the type of material the comic is working on. If your intention is to perform a G-rated act, any suggestions for X-rated punch lines won't be helpful in reaching your goal.

The person running the workshop should have the experience to guide you in the right direction and help mold your individual style so it has a better chance to work on a comedy stage. His opinion should carry a lot of weight, but he shouldn't pretend to have all the answers or the final say on what you "must" do. Members of the workshop can also offer thoughts, punch lines, bits, and other ideas based on what they see and hear. This will lead to discovering a unique and productive way for the comic to write, and influence how the material could be handled on stage.

Performance techniques such as delivery, pauses, callbacks, destroying hecklers, and even how to handle a microphone can be valuable advice for new comedians. This often helps give the performer confidence, a more professional stage presentation, and insight into the comedy world. But the best "teacher" will always be the audience, and one way to prepare for an audience can be through the supportive environment of a good workshop.

After locating a workshop near you (or a few dozen if you live in New York City or Los Angeles), talk with the person running it. Ask what is offered and if it's geared for someone starting out in the business. You might run across workshops for comedians who already have stage experience that might include how a certain club wants MCs to host their shows or the business aspects of promoting a career. These are topics serious performers will eventually learn through trial and error, by getting generous advice from comics they work with, or by attending workshops in the style of a lecture with questions, answers, and examples of promotional material, contracts, and other information about the business.

It's much easier to find a workshop aimed for beginners. But before you choose one, find out how many people will be involved, keeping in mind, the smaller the better. In my experience, workshops limiting the amount of participants means the person running it plans on giving everyone individual attention. As I've mentioned, comedy is a very personal craft and each comic needs to keep his own sense of humor while developing a personal writing technique and performing style.

It's important for the organizer to give his attention to everyone on an individual basis. In other words, he shouldn't bite off more than he can chew. This also has to do with the amount of time the class meets. You can't give ten people as much attention in two hours as you can in four.

On a personal note, I took a comedy class and a comedy workshop in New York City before deciding to get into this business. Both were completely different experiences, with one being much more valuable than the other.

The class left me feeling as if the school only wanted my money. There were approximately twenty people in a ten-week course that met two hours each week. This didn't leave us with a lot of individual performing time, because each of us was required to do a short act at every session. We met in a classroom, not a comedy club, and took turns standing in front of the group reciting a three-minute routine without a microphone or any interruptions. When we finished, the "teacher," while never getting out of his chair to make a point or demonstrate any thoughts about our delivery, would be the only person to make a few comments about the material before quickly moving on to his next victim. The sad part was that he didn't even bother to learn our names, which was very evident in the class and also when he ran into any of us venturing into a comedy club.

The workshop setting was a much better experience. The group was limited to ten people and had a waiting list, which is always a good indication the person in charge wasn't packing in as many people as possible to make more money. We met at a comedy club and had use of a stage and microphone; the workshop instructor helped us work on our material without ever actually writing it for us. He wasn't shy about telling us what was and wasn't funny, asking the other participants for suggestions, or getting on stage and demonstrating how a different delivery could make the act better.

After each meeting he expected us to use our talent and ability to improve the act before doing it again the next week. We only met a few productive times before being introduced to our real "teacher," a paying audience, which happened when we walked on stage to do our three-minute sets. Throw in the fact that the workshop instructor also knew our names, and it was enough to get me hooked.

If you don't have a comedy act, a good workshop will help you start the process of developing one. But here's a little bit of advice: Most people getting into comedy have already imagined being on stage and talking about . . . well, something. I doubt I'm going out on a limb by thinking you already have ideas.

Start early by putting these thoughts together before going to the first meeting of a workshop. Whether it's only a few ideas jotted down in a notebook, a funny conversation, personal experience, or any humorous opinions you want to discuss. Pick a topic from all that information and be prepared to talk about it in front of the group. This will put you ahead of the game, rather than starting from scratch.

This advice is based on a technique used in many workshops when someone claims he doesn't have any material. When he's coaxed into talking about what interests him, more often than not something funny will come out. He may not realize it, but the others in the group will when they hear it. Even if the laughs aren't there yet, an outside observer (with that important creative mind) can usually help in finding some potential for humor within the subject. This is always a good starting point to help new performers develop a comedy routine.

One thing I say too much in my workshops is that we're not performing brain surgery. It's comedy and basically meant to be funny and entertaining. If the material is insightful or enlightening (George Carlin), that's a plus. If it's just about nothing except being funny, (the sitcom *Seinfeld*, which was the writers' admission, not mine), that's just as good!

Also keep in mind you'll never meet a successful comedian who claims the first thing he ever did on a comedy stage was his best performance ever. Quite often, material offered at the first meeting of a workshop is eventually rewritten or never done again as you continue to grow as both a writer and performer. A good comic will always be searching for new material and ways to improve his on-stage delivery. Writing and performing a comedy act is an individual process and a good workshop is meant to be a launching pad to get your act onto a comedy stage where it belongs.

Eddie Brill (Comedian Talent Coordinator for Late Show with David Letterman)

I would make sure the person [running the workshop] was patient, compassionate, and really cared about teaching. That's the main thing about a workshop. If a workshop is to work, it has to be a situation where everyone is learning and teaching together. You know, when I do a workshop, I'm not the only teacher. Everyone in the class is a teacher, as well. So I recommend it, but you have to be very careful. There are a lot of workshops and comedy classes out there that are run by incompetent people and they give you very bad advice. They're really out to only make the money. And there are some pretty big ones out there, especially in New York where it's all about money and nothing else. And although that's what life is about, it's not the thing you want to get out of a workshop.

Experience counts. Also the ability to be a good teacher. There are a lot of people who are very talented, but cannot teach. They're not compassionate with people. They don't have patience.

The important thing is for the workshop to be very honest and egoless. Because the only way you'll ever learn is by getting the truth—and the truth isn't always pretty. But you must be willing to leave your ego at the door and learn. And your teacher must be willing to learn, as well.

FAQ 5 What's the Deal with Open Mikes?

I performed at my first open mike last night and don't know what to make of the experience. I was pretty nervous, but had written some jokes and decided it was time to do this. There were ten other comics and four regular customers sitting at the bar. By the time I did my set, all but two of the comics had already performed and left. I did my five minutes and the other comics told me it wasn't bad for someone doing it for the first time. I didn't think the manager had been listening at all, so I was surprised that he said I could come back again—which made me feel pretty good. But the people at the bar talked the whole time and were more interested in the television.

It wasn't the big rush like I expected and I wasn't that nervous because nobody seemed to pay much attention to me. Is this typical? —J.B.

Welcome to the entrance ramp for the road to comedy success. Hopefully, your journey through "The Wonderful World of Open Mikes" won't be too long, but expect some bumps, potholes, construction, detours, tolls, and unpredictable traveling companions along the way. There are no posted speed limits, but also no shortcuts that I know of. The idea is to try and maintain control, be observant, and learn from your success and failures, while always keeping your destination within sight.

Open-mike clubs (or open-mike rooms, as they're known in "the biz") can be described in two ways: undergraduate classroom or a necessary evil.

Either way, they're important venues where comedians can lay the ground-work for a future career in comedy or a return to their regular lives in "the real world."

Typically, an open mike will not pay performers. In fact, when you figure in your personal time, traveling expenses, and whatever food or beverage you purchase with the hope of impressing a club manager,booker, or bartender, it'll cost you to perform. Consider it tuition, or if you're allowed to run a food and beverage bill to be paid later, a college loan.

Each open mike is different, just like an audience. Some can be plush nightclubs with a large crowd (usually enticed by a happy hour or free food), which are excellent places to try material and gain on-stage experi-ence. Others might be dingy bars with patrons (if there are any), calling for you to "keep it down" so they can hear the television. In between these bookend examples is where you'll spend most of your time as a beginning comic. And if you look at open mikes for what they're meant to be, it should be time well spent.

The reasons behind going to open mikes are simple. It's where you'll put together an act and make it presentable (funny) for future audiences. You'll try new ideas, throw out bad ones, and generally learn how to write and perform. It's possible to create funny material and perform it in front of a mirror in your apartment or for your friends, but it's a different "Wonderful World" standing in front of a spotlight and talking into a microphone for a group of people who expect to be entertained. This is hands-on experience and like any job or internship, there's no way to get better at it than by rolling up your sleeves and getting to work.

It's important to use any performance opportunity to your advantage. When there's an audience, learn what it takes to make them laugh. If there are only a few other comics listening, make them laugh (believe me, they'll be your toughest audience). If no one is paying attention or you're playing to one drunk passed out at the bar (typical 4 AM set, learned from personal experience), consider it a practice session and a chance to say your act out loud.

Because they represent a starting point, open-mike rooms give comedians no where else to go but up *if* they're intent on using their talent, dedication, and desire to get better. Make every performance a learning experience. With time, you'll eventually get off this bumpy road and into real comedy clubs where the adventure truly starts.

Did You Hear The One About . . . ?

- **Bringer Shows.** Sometimes owners of open-mike rooms aren't concerned about how funny the comedians are. They're more worried about having an audience so the club stays in business. One way of generating finances is to require each performer to bring a certain number of paying customers if they want to get on stage that night. Though it's a major complaint for many comics and a measure of loyal support by family and friends who are asked again and again to help fill the requirement, it's an early lesson in the true meaning of show *business*.

- **Cattle Call.** Did I mention that a lot of people attempt comedy for a lot of different reasons? Of course it's a passion for some, therapy for others, or a hobby for the adventurous looking for more excitement than a crocheting class. Actors may view comedy as a chance for Hollywood exposure, novices as a fast track to riches and fame, or unemployed accountants as a career alternative. Comedy attracts all types, and chances are you'll see them *all* at open mikes, auditions, and venues where the only requirement needed to perform is to just show up. This term traditionally refers to the acting and dancing side of the entertainment industry when an "open call" would attract hundreds, even thousands of hopefuls to a single audition. Gazing at the long lines and crowded waiting areas, you can almost imagine a cowboy appearing through a dusty sunset to open the gates and herd everyone in. No doubt it'll be a long night.

- **Bumped.** Imagine it's the seventh game of the World Series. Tie score and the home team is batting in the ninth inning, with two out and nobody on base. Suddenly the hitter connects and the historic ball is flying toward the center field bleachers where you just happen to be seated. As you jump up to catch the home run that will put you in every highlight film for years to come, a bigger guy knocks you out of the way and makes the grab. Your excuse is that you were "bumped." This is similar to how it works in the comedy world. You have a scheduled time to perform, but someone with a bigger name shows up unannounced, and the club manager puts him on stage instead of you. The manager's excuse? "You've been bumped."

Mark Curry

My experience with open-mike clubs was "crash and kill." You know? Whenever I got up there, I tried to kill the club. If it was a minute, two minutes, three minutes—I would try to kill them as long as possible. If I saw the light come on, I always acted like I didn't see it. And the club owner would never mind, as long as they were laughing.

I was in Oakland and it was rough. I started doing rap concerts, before I started doing comedy clubs. They wouldn't let me in the clubs. I started doing, you know, 15–20,000 people at rap shows before I even went to a club. It was open-mikes to rap concerts and then clubs.

There really were no open mikes. The open mikes were where you created them. And open mike was literally, where you took a microphone and you opened it up! No matter where the hell it was. It could be at a club, it could be at a barbeque. It didn't make no difference where it was. It was just an "open mike." It was a mike and you picked it up and you did your thing.

It didn't have to be a club, it could be anywhere. You couldn't get into the big clubs. It was impossible. So wherever you could, you know, whether it be a little dinky club that had a band . . . Wherever there was a mike, I picked it up. Wherever there were people.

FAQ 6 How Do I Get to Perform at Open Mikes?

Do I need to know someone with a connection, like the owner or another comic? Would I just show up and say I want to perform? I've never done comedy before, but I've written some jokes and practiced in front of my friends. I think it's time for me to do this. How long do they let you perform? —C.S.

Getting on stage at an open mike is easier than getting a taxi in New York City during rush hour, passing through airport security with a metal plate in your head, or asking your friends to pay a cover charge to see you perform a set they've already paid to see at least a dozen times before. Then again, it's also a little more difficult than just walking into a club, grabbing the microphone, and launching into your full-length one-person show.

Finding opportunities on stage as a new comedian can often be time-consuming and sometimes disappointing. Locating open mikes where you can perform is only the first step. After that you must follow the club's policy for a performance spot.

The best situation is when you can confirm a date in advance by phone. But as the new kid on the block there's no guarantee you won't get "bumped" if the local open-mike star wanders in unannounced—especially if he's a friend of the person in charge. In many cases where a comedian is running the show, "a friend" can be someone who also has an open mike, and they trade stage time at their clubs.

Does this give you an idea? Good. Don't lose that thought because we'll come back to it in a few moments. . . .

Other open mikes can make you feel like the subject of *Dumb and Dumber.* The management will schedule a certain time (say, noon on Mondays), when they'll take a select number of phone calls from comics who can sign up to perform. Did you ever try to win free concert tickets by being the tenth caller to a radio station? This is pretty much the same thing. You call at the designated time and keep hitting the redial button hoping to be one of the lucky winners. If it's a popular club, keep a sandwich nearby because it might be a long process. If you get through, go out and buy a lottery ticket because it's your lucky day.

Then again, if it's your phone that's ringing off the hook at the designated hour . . . Well, hang onto that thought also.

The comedy lottery can also be a long shot, but it's actually a very fair method of choosing who gets the coveted open mike and audition spots in the more popular clubs. When I managed The Original Improv in New York City, we scheduled auditions for the first Sunday of every month. Since most comedians in the area dreamed of performing on the famous stage, it was not uncommon for the line of hopefuls waiting for their chance to stretch to the end of the block on West Forty-Fourth Street and around the corner along Ninth Avenue.

The doors to The Improv would open at 5:00 PM and everyone would cram in or stand outside by the windows to hear the selection policy. As each comic entered, they would sign a notebook with their name and phone number, then wait to be called in groups of five. The nerve-racking process would continue as they were led to a roped-off area where I was holding a champagne bucket filled with small pieces of folded paper. If one hundred comics were there (which was not uncommon), the bucket would hold eighty-five blank pieces, while the remaining ones would be numbered one through fifteen. Since only fifteen three-minute audition spots were available during that night's show, eighty-five people would leave disappointed and have to wait until the next month's audition.

As my dad always said about the lottery, "You can't win unless you play." The same optimism also can hold true in the comedy lottery. But if you're consistently out of luck, the signed notebook can be your winning ticket. If The Improv had written proof a comedian had signed-up to audition six months in a row without getting on stage, he'd be rewarded with a spot that night. Nothing's ever fair in love and war, but comedy can sometimes have a soft heart.

Some open mikes practice the show business technique known as the cattle call. Again, there is a designated time to sign-up for a performance spot, but you must be at the club, in person, to take advantage of it. The management may only take the first ten comics in line, which means you should take a portable chair and reading material, and plan to get there early if it's a popular club. If you arrive and see you're number eleven, set your alarm clock earlier for the next opportunity and try again.

When the hours of the show permit, there are open mikes that will give everyone who attends a performance spot. This can be done on a first-come, first-serve basis, or as a lottery with estimated performance times picked at random. I've been to clubs in New York that will start the show at 7 P.M. and run until 4 A.M. with a continuous stream of comics. The comics would arrive at 6 P.M. to pick a time and often find themselves either going home, to a movie, taking a nap, or performing at another open mike before returning to do their spot.

As far as the time limit for your first performances, expect to be on stage for three to five minutes. If you get laughs from the audience and management decides you deserve extra time on stage, they'll let you know by inviting you back for another show. Eventually you could be offered much longer sets, but remember, it's a gradual process as you build confidence in your material and performance ability.

Now, if you still have the thoughts I asked you to hang onto earlier, we'll get to those in a moment. But first . . .

Brett Butler

A lot's changed since I began comedy over twenty years ago: venues, media, and nearly every aspect of the business. What hasn't changed is that people will always want to see a good comedian. In terms of getting stage time, I recommend getting a good set of blinders. It's none of my business who else goes on where, how much they get, or who comes in first in contests. If I focus on material, delivery, and, most important, that real "voice" that's only mine, the rest seems to sort itself out. Of course we don't get into this business by being the most balanced of individuals and it's only natural to compare art, acts, progress, and accolades with other comedians. I have never regretted keeping my eyes on "my own paper."

My favorite comedians do the same thing. We know a secret: It all works out the way it's supposed to. But you have to be as old as me to finally realize it.

FAQ 7   How Would I Go about Running My Own Open Mike?

I'm thinking about starting my own open-mike room because it would give me a regular place to work on my act. There's a bar near me that might go for this and it wouldn't be a problem getting other comics. How do I go about setting this up? What kind of equipment would I need and how would I advertise this? Would I pay the owner to let me do this or would he pay me? Any advice would be appreciated. —M.M.

I knew earlier there'd be a reason to drop hints even Austin Powers couldn't miss . . .

If you're looking for a part-time job with salary paid in stage time, running your own open mike is not a bad idea. The benefits don't include medical (for the headaches), company car (to get you there), or paid vacations (when you just need a night off), but if you're determined to have regular stage experience to get your comedy career off the ground, this is a good way to break into the business.

The best scenario for running an open mike is to find a nightclub or bar with a built-in audience starved for entertainment. The owner should already have a stage with lights, sound system, and be eager to hang a sign in the window saying "Open Mike Tonight," which would, of course, be a magnet for funny acts, hungry to perform. Your job would be to decide who performs and when, while getting your fill of stage time.

Unfortunately, that's not very likely to happen. In reality, you'll have to convince a club owner who is hungry for customers to try an open-mike night—with you handling all the details.

At least you won't have to worry about filling out tax forms at the end of the year, since your profit will most likely be the time you spend on stage. And if the club owner is looking for you to foot any part of the bill, keep searching until you find one a little more hungry.

The bottom line is that a club owner will not do anything that will lose money. He may give a new concept a trial run with the hope it pays off in the future, but economics will have the final say. Therefore, your first step is to convince him that an open mike will bring in more customers who will spend more money in his establishment.

Once you've accomplished this, start working with what the club already has available, what the owner is willing to provide, or what you need to supply. If the club is already equipped with a stage, lights, and microphone with a sound system, you're halfway there. If not, you'll have to start from scratch.

To work, a performance space has to look like a performance space. If there's not a stage, either build a small one or designate an area in the room where the acts can perform. This location should be the main focus in the club during the shows and visible to as many customers as possible.

If you're familiar with more traditional comedy clubs, you'll notice that the first row of tables and chairs are usually placed near the stage. Think of the old Vaudeville routine when an audience member in the front row is resting his foot on the stage:

Performer: "Are you in show business?"
Audience member: "No."
Performer: "Then get your foot off the stage!"

The rest of the seating is arranged as tight as city fire codes will allow. The reasons for tight seating arrangement are simple:

One reason is that laughter is contagious. It's much easier to laugh out loud as part of a group, which is beneficial for both the audience and performers.

Also, many comedians don't enjoy performing for an audience that is seated too far away. Their close proximity to the stage makes the shows more intimate, personal, and gives the comics an opportunity to "get-in-their-faces," if that happens to be their style. Do your best to arrange the room in this manner, and the audience will have a clue they're at a show and not just hanging around in a nightclub.

Stage lighting is another way to keep everyone's focus on the performers. From personal experience, this can be done inexpensively and effectively—and is worth the effort.

Since I doubt we're talking about lighting up Yankee Stadium or the Hollywood Bowl, don't be too concerned about having high-tech lights. Many discount and appliance stores carry small spotlights or lamps that are hung over workbenches or used when tooling under cars. They have a clip-on feature and can be attached to poles or hung onto whatever is available so the light will shine on the area where it's needed. Buy one or two of these and aim them toward the stage. When it's showtime, just plug them in and you'll be the spotlight of attention.

A sound system is basically a microphone with a stand and an amplifier with a speaker. For my first open mike, I bought a very small guitar amplifier that was not even two feet high or wide. Used, it cost less than $100. We placed it in front of the microphone to avoid "feedback" (a musical technique that allows guitar players to feel like Jimi Hendrix) and turned up the volume. Nobody in the room missed a word.

After setting up a usable performance space in the club, you can just sit back and wait for audiences to flock in for your open mike shows—correct? If you think so, you need to wake up because you're dreaming about that best-case scenario again. . . .

The next move is to turn yourself into a publicist. It's important to let potential customers know you're running a show they *have* to see. If the club owner will agree to pay for advertising, whether it's in the local newspapers or radio, start writing promotional copy. You should also check if any newspapers carry free listings for entertainment and get the information—where, when, and cost of admission—to them at least one to two weeks before the show. (Word of advice: check with the listings' editor for deadlines and don't be late.)

Flyers also are a simple and effective tool when advertising your shows. Anyone with basic computer skills can type out a one-page promotional flyer and make copies. Pass them out to friends, co-workers, acquaintances, and anyone you think might be interested in a comedy show. If your open mike is in a high-pedestrian area, stand outside and hand them to people walking by. If you're into delegating, ask a few comedians to take on that assignment in exchange for stage time.

When it comes to advertising, use your imagination and have fun—as you continue to work hard. When you get an audience, the best promotion is to give them a great show. Good word-of-mouth could result in a regular clientele, a happy club owner and an experienced comic—you!

Jackie "The Joke Man" Martling

I was in a three-piece band called The Off-Hour Rockers. We told dirty jokes and played our own songs. We were very wild and funny, but there was no place for us to go. At one point, the other two guys said, "Jackie, we're leaving the band." Now, I'm no rocket scientist, but if there's three guys in the band and two of them leave, that's kicking me out of the band!

I started toying around with comedy after I ran into some stand-ups at a gig we were all working together. I just started hanging around with them and they used to come down when I was playing solo nights in clubs. Guys like Eddie Murphy and Bob Nelson. They'd come over to get stage time where I was playing and we'd work together whenever we could. You know, we'd make five dollars a night, ten dollars a night . . . whatever.

Since I had been a guitar player in bands, I had an amplifier, speakers, and a microphone with a stand. So, bingo—I was a producer. I put on shows and would charge the club owner, pay the comics, and host the shows or do a spot at the end.

FAQ 8 Open Mikes: Been There, Done That. What's the Next Step?

I'm really getting frustrated with open mikes, but know I need more experience before auditioning at real comedy clubs. I can't keep asking my friends to go as paid audience members (so I can get on stage), because they've seen me too many times already. There's a couple I can go to every week, but the only audience they ever get are other comics waiting to go on. I'm not getting ahead in this business and it's starting to get to me. Any ideas? —A.K.

Here's my impression of an annoying infomercial pitchman. You know the type of guy I'm talking about—the high-energy salesman offering you, "A proven method that could change your life. It's so simple that you'll be frustrated you didn't think of it first. It'll kick-start your career, save your friends from unconsciously memorizing your act, and give you experience real comedy clubs are looking for!"

Are you interested? Then read the following in an announcer's loud and fast voice:

> Don't touch that dial! We'll be right back after an important message from our sponsor. Are you tired of bringer shows? Tired of arriving early only to get a late performance spot? Are you fed-up with relying on sheer luck to get on stage? Even if you're running an open mike one or two nights a week, are you frustrated that you are not performing on a more regular basis? Then check out our new feature, Other Open Mike Options!

1. Find out what organizations or clubs in your area are doing events or benefits. Then volunteer to be the host—free of charge! There's a reason why professional speakers use humor in their presentations. It keeps the audience attentive and entertained at the same time. Your sense of humor can make introductions, announcements, and award ceremonies from becoming boring, without cutting into a budget usually aimed for food and beverages. Better still, as a marketing tool, tell them you'll donate your standard fee for whatever it is they're organized to do. Even if your actual fee is less than a bag of potato chips, make up a figure and tell them to keep it. You may even get listed as a contributor!

2. Everybody wants to be a star, which is the basic idea behind karaoke—the imported Japanese art of removing a professional singer's voice from a popular song and allowing anyone who can't tune an air-guitar to sing the lead. Sign up for karaoke performance spot and when it's your turn, ask to do a few minutes of stand-up instead. The patrons might appreciate the break from the evening's assault on their eardrums and depending on the next singer's choice of songs, you could walk out saying you opened for Cher or The Village People.

3. Takin' It to the Streets. Street corner comedy is not uncommon in New York City, the beaches near Los Angeles, or in almost any city with a lot

of pedestrian traffic. It's good advice to find out if a permit is needed to perform, but otherwise the only requirements are a desire to get better and to acquire nerves of steel. Get a few other like-minded and brave comics to rotate sets and launch into a show. You'll soon have an audience, more comedy experience, and if anyone has a knack for finances and remembers to pass a hat, possibly enough money to inspire a second show.

4. This is pure genius, but unfortunately I can't take credit for it. When confronted with a bringer show and an exhausted list of friends and relatives, New York comedian Chris Murphy printed flyers advertising the evening's open-mike show. He stood outside the club and handed them to people walking by until the magic number he needed had paid admission and were seated inside. He gave the leftover flyers to another comedian in the same situation, then walked on stage and performed for his "brought" audience.

Chris Murphy

I call it guerilla warfare. You know, Viet Cong kinda comedy. A lot of times if you're inexperienced, people aren't going to come see you. But if you're handing out flyers you have a guaranteed audience, which is something you can't do on your own because you don't draw. You don't have a "name" yet.

It works in New York especially, because there are so many funny comics. Why would someone hire you when there are comics better than you? What can you do for them? Well, you need to bring in a crowd. If you can't bring in a crowd with your name, you can make a name for yourself with the club owners by handing out flyers.

It's kind of a cool thing to do, but I didn't make it up. They were doing it at The Boston Comedy Club in New York City. Then I took it and went to a club we started. That's how we got a lot of people in there.

I handed out flyers for a year and a half. Once I passed my audition at The Improv, I spoke to the manager of The Boston Comedy Club and asked if I could start doing Mondays there without handing out flyers. I made my bones at Boston and doing open mikes, then used the experience to pass at The Improv. Then I used the fact that I played Boston and The Improv to pass at The New York Comedy Club. Suddenly, I was a regular at three clubs. But it was the reputation of The Improv and the stage time I got from handing out flyers that got me into those places.

In order to pass at a major club, you have to have others think you're funny first— before the owner will make a move on you. No one likes to risk the first move by saying someone is funny. It has to come from a bunch of people, preferably from comedians who are funny and respected. And the best way to get around bringer shows is other comics' recommendations. Best way to get their recommendation is to be funny. Best way to be funny is to go on wherever people let you!

Comics stopped handing out flyers for a long time and now all of a sudden, the kids are doing it again. But make sure the people in the book know I haven't done this since 1990. I don't want them to think I'm a hundred years old and handing out flyers!

Al Martin (owner, numerous comedy clubs)

Find a way to make yourself as useful as possible to the club. Are you a printer? Are you a carpenter? Are you an electrician or a plumber? Any one of those skills that can be helpful to a club could be used to barter for stage time. I have not, in all the years I've been in comedy, been able to find a plumber. I've had electricians up the ying-yang. I've had carpenters, dentists, lawyers . . . I've had every kind of stuff done, except it's hard to find a plumber.

FAQ 9 Help! How Do I Overcome Writer's Block?

I've been having writer's block lately and finding it really hard to come up with any material. When I do have an idea, I can only take it so far and then I lose the humor. I want to make comedy work for me, because it's the best high I've ever had (and I did some major pot in my younger days). —S.B.

What writer's block? Your last line seems to have comedy potential, even for audiences who can actually remember their younger days or think "munchies" are characters in a video game. It's just too bad I can't think of anything else to write about the subject . . . Not!!

You must realize that once you decide to become a comedian, you are writing material from that moment on. This is an on-going process, which should be happening all the time. Everything you do, say, think, hear, and see has the potential of becoming comedy material. The sources are endless and include conversations, observations, television, the Internet, newspapers, magazines—just about anything that gets your attention. The opportunity to find comedy is all around you and it's important to "tune in."

Successful comedians know how to think funny. The confident ones (and that's not a bad trait for success) can dig into almost any topic in an attempt to find some humor in it. Even if the end result isn't funny, it can still be an exercise in writing.

I read an interview with the late George Harrison in which he was asked about writing songs. He explained that he would "doodle" on the guitar, then out of nowhere would come a song. It's the same with comedy. If you look for the "funny" and keep notes of your thoughts, eventually you'll have enough ideas to "doodle" with and possibly develop into solid material. It probably won't all be good, but with a little work it shouldn't all be bad either. It takes patience, dedication, and having the right frame of mind.

Examine your daily life; family, job, hobbies, what you watch on television or even what got you into comedy in the first place. What are your thoughts about what's going on in the world? It can be almost *anything*. Then look for the humor—*your* humor—within it. Why did you think it was funny enough to share with an audience in the first place?

For example, let's say you have a great premise for a joke or a bit. You may have seen something potentially funny on a trip to the mall, such as a guy following his wife while holding all her shopping bags. Since you're tuned in to your humor radar, make notes on why you thought it was funny (his expression, the amount of bags, the way he walked, etc.), and take time to think about it. What actually happened or what do you imagine could have happened? Were you or someone you know ever in a similar situation? Is there someone else in the mall you could compare him to? Was there anything in the news about the differences between men and women, carrying heavy loads, shopping tips, the benefits or stress of spending time together as a couple? How would you immediately describe this situation to someone else in a funny way?

Use all these real and imagined premises and start adding your opinions and humor. Because you're now a comedy writer and need to work at it to improve your craft, set a goal each day to create a few different endings for the bit or add new ideas and descriptions. If the material seems to be coming together, then continue polishing it. If not, put it away and work on something else. If you come back to the bit because it seems to still have potential, it could be worth putting in more effort. If it doesn't, consider it writing practice and dedicate the same effort to another topic. If nothing else, you might come up with a good bit on how hard it is to write material about guys carrying packages in a mall.

Since I can't overemphasize that comedians have an individual voice, presence, or character on stage, perhaps you're the type of person who can separate himself from you—the performer. If that's the case, then write for *that* person. What would you want that particular performer to talk about? If you're a sympathetic person on stage, come at it from that angle. If you're a hard hitter with a sarcastic edge, drop a verbal nuclear bomb on the subject. I know this is getting a whole out-of-body theme going (in fact, I could use some munchies right now), but look at your favorite comedian or musician. If you were going to see them, what subjects would you expect them to talk about or what type of songs would you want to hear? Consider who you are on stage and look for material that would fit that out-of-body thought pattern.

I'd also like to point out that I practice what I preach. I personally understand the worries about writer's block and coming up with material because I've been there myself and have learned how to work through it.

By tuning in to my personal thoughts, observations, and humor, I've been able to write an 800-word newspaper humor column every week for a number of years. It can sometimes be tough coming up with topics and meeting a deadline, but I've learned to relax and think about newsworthy events or what I had personally seen, heard, or experienced during the week. There are many false starts while trying to get something on paper, but once I get an idea it becomes a matter of dedicating the time and effort to see where it leads. If it doesn't work, I go through the process again. Sooner or later, with the correct mind-set, I'll find something funny to keep myself (and hopefully readers), interested enough so I'm still employed to do it all over again the next week.

Richard Jeni

I found that everybody has a peak creative time of the day. I researched it and found out that mine is between 5:00 and 5:02 every morning. So what I do is set my alarm for 5:00 and I write down the first thing that comes into my mind. As a result, I have a lot of jokes that begin, "God, I really have to pee. . . ." So it's not a foolproof method, but it helps me to keep coming up with stuff.

What's That Mean?

- **Tune In.** A comedian's mind is like a computer hard drive. To develop more comedy material while on stage or to even comment on what might be happening in the showroom during a performance, that hard drive must be turned on. In other words, the comic must listen, watch, and pay attention to his thoughts and surroundings. Tune in, turn on . . . but be funny.

- **Premise.** An idea for a joke, bit, or comedy monologue. It's another term for the proverbial light bulb flashing on over a comic's head when they think to themselves, "Hey, that's funny!"

- **A Bit.** A segment, piece, or chunk of a comedy routine. Length and subject doesn't matter. If a comedian is going to talk about his car, it could be a one-liner or his entire set for that night. When he gets off stage, he can say, "I did my car bit."

- **Riffing.** Having a topic and verbally developing it into a comedy bit by using whatever thoughts it generates in your mind at that moment. To use musical terms, it's a jam session in your head and you're trying to come up with a piece everyone can follow. You hope something worthwhile comes out (in comedy terms, it's called "funny"), and the technique relies on your natural talent to create comedy on the spot.

- **A Hook.** A fisherman has one at the end of his line when he's trying to catch a fish. A comedian can have verbal lines or physical traits within his comedy routine that will catch an audience's attention and keep it. The individual possibilities are endless, as long as it fits the comedian's image or material. For example, he could be known as "only the husband" or "the guy with the pet dinosaur." He may regularly claim to "know it all" or "I know nothing about it, but this is how I see it." The audience will become familiar with the performer's style and if they like it, he'll reel them in for laughs and return engagements. The most famous "hook" award goes to Jeff Foxworthy for, "You might be a redneck . . ." But for another one that's running "neck-to-neck" in the popularity polls. . . .

Bill Engvall

I've been doing "Here's Your Sign" for years. I used to say that stupid people should be slapped. But one day my wife said, "You know, that's kinda harsh." So one night in a club, I believe it was in Omaha of all places, I kinda started dickin' around with it and came up with this "sign" bit. And it hooked in. In fact, I used to sell those little signs for a dollar apiece—or two for five bucks—and it would just say, "I'm stupid." And people would buy 'em. I'd sell out of them. I mean, it was amazing.

I'd say somebody would do something stupid and you'd slap them, and go POW! But when I started to do the sign, I turned it into saying, "If they had to wear these signs, then you wouldn't rely on them. You wouldn't ask them, you'd see them. Then when they did something, you'd just go, 'Here's your sign.'" And that was it. That was what caught everybody's attention.

When we were putting (my first) album together, we were trying to decide on a title. My manager said, "Why don't you just call it 'Here's Your Sign.'" And I was like, "Yeah. All right." I was trying to come up with something really cool and all of a sudden, you know, here it was right in front of me. Sometimes you need that person there to . . . It's like the old saying, "You don't see the forest for the trees." Because I was so into it, but . . . didn't . . . And God, who knew? Man, who knew "Here's Your Sign" was gonna . . . That one put me over the top.

Brian Regan

I try not to be too easily defined. If I start hearing comments like, "Oh, you're the guy who always feels stupid," or something like that, then I start writing away from that.

I guess some people spend their whole career trying to find a hook. I try to find a way to get out of being involved with a hook. I want to be able to talk about anything and everything. I don't want to be tied down to some easily identifiable type of comedian. I try to explore all different kinds of things, so it's fun.

Obviously, other comedians have gotten huge benefits from going that route. So I don't have any negative comments about it. I just prefer not to do that.

But this topic fascinates me because there's a whole other thing going on. You see it especially with the comics out in Los Angeles. Everyone is being encouraged to write "an act" that is driven around a character that can easily be put into a sitcom. Either as the main character or as a peripheral character, and I just have absolutely refused to follow suit.

I've had advice from people over the last ten years going, "You know, you gotta have 'an act,' so when the network executives come and watch it, they'll go, 'Oh, I get it! I can see that as a show.'"

And it's like, I refuse. I refuse! Because I love the art of stand-up too much to be doing it purely as a vehicle to make things easier for network executives. I love being a stand-up. I think it's an art form. And it might sound self-serving, because now I'm, in a way, suggesting I'm an artist, but I think it is an art form. And I think we comedians should be able to explore what we want to explore on stage. And to see all these comedians doing what are clearly these little characters that can be put into sitcoms just . . . I don't know. I'm not a fan of that.

FAQ 10 How Am I Gonna Memorize All These Lines?

Any ideas or tips for memorizing material? I've gotten into just rereading the things I've written over and over, but would like your comments. —J.W.

After rereading your question a few times, I felt confident I could go outside and repeat it to my neighbor. Well, maybe not exactly, but I could get the point across. It really shouldn't matter what order the words come out, as long as my neighbor understands what I'm saying. If I have his attention and get the desired reaction, the message has been delivered.

Memorizing an act is often a safety net for new comedians. There's nothing wrong with knowing your material word for word in an exact order if it helps builds enough confidence to get you on stage. The key to this technique is not having it sound memorized. A great delivery can even give an old joke new life, so practice hard at making your material sound spontaneous (like you're making it up on the spot), and conversational.

Unless you're cut from the "no fear" mold of comics who would only consider using a safety net as a prop rather than to stop a fall (think Carrot Top), everyone can be different when it comes to preparing their act for the stage. Some will memorize it and do the routine exactly the same way every time.

Others will let it flow around a mental outline of topics, a knowledge of where the jokes or descriptions need to be delivered within the set, or based on how they feel at that particular moment. The important thing is to make your comic points during the set and not let it sound as if you're repeating a memorized script.

Since there are always exceptions to any rule, one might be if a key element in your delivery is the humor that comes from performing a memorized routine. An example would be a commercial parody where the comic is lampooning a familiar radio or television advertisement. He could use an announcer's voice and the exact wording each time to give it the necessary comic punch:

> *I eat cat food every day because it's not only good for me, but it keeps my hair shiny and manageable. Try Jim's Cat Food. It's purr-fect.*

For a while, it seemed too many acts were writing song parodies based on "The Brady Bunch Theme Song." To make it work, they had to sing the familiar tune with new lyrics fitting the exact musical beat:

> *"Here's a story, about a man named Brady . . ."* might become,
> *"I eat cat food, 'cuz it makes me purr-fect . . ."*

Admittedly, I'm no Weird Al when it comes to song parodies, but the humor is based on the comical lyrics fitting the melody. And even though some comics can't carry a tune (which can be funny in itself), the song would be performed the exact same way each time because the pre-written words make it work.

In a case like this, you would have to keep practicing until you had it memorized. Think of how many times you heard "The Brady Bunch Theme Song" before knowing all the words, and you can estimate how long it might take you to recite your bit from memory.

If you have a difficult time memorizing or doing your routine without it sounding memorized, try going on stage with only an outline for the act in your head. You can even write the key words in a notebook and take it on stage with you for a reference. Acknowledge to the audience that you have a "cheat sheet," or whatever you prefer to call it so they don't look at you as a total amateur (it's part of "being aware" of what goes on in the room), and look at it only when you need to. I've seen Jay Leno take a notebook on stage at the Los Angeles Improv because he wanted to work on new monologue jokes. He never actually read an entire bit off it, but glanced at key words in case his performance went off into a different direction, and he wanted to get back to what he had planned to talk about. The important thing is to be comfortable knowing where the laughs or punch lines should be and don't forget to deliver them.

Know the basic joke, or point of the line or story you want to make. Then get there as you would if you were telling it to a group of friends at a party. That's an example used quite often in my workshops. If someone is struggling to remember his material exactly as he had written it or appears nervous, I remind him that a comedy club is supposed to be a fun place. People are there to laugh and if you mess up, so what? If you're good-natured about it and are having fun yourself, the audience will pick up on that feeling and hopefully follow along. Your mistakes could turn into very funny moments and possibly lead the material in a direction you hadn't thought of before.

There was a comic in one of my workshops who would simply go ballistic on stage during our sessions when he couldn't remember his material word for word. Each time he messed up, he would either throw himself on the floor, pound the wall in frustration, or throw up his hands and declare he was a screw up who will never get it right. It was an example of his true emotions and since he never actually hurt himself, the tirades were hysterically funny to all of us who were watching.

We urged him (begged might be a better word), to keep these honest feelings in his act. It gave his delivery a raw, spontaneous feeling that made him unpredictable, edgy, and in the moment. The energy level brought a new life to his written material and his body language was both powerful and almost slapstick. It made him a real presence on the stage.

The problem was that he didn't believe us. He saw his forgetfulness as a roadblock to success and wanted to make his routine as perfect as possible. After some constant begging from the rest of us, he finally agreed to let his true emotions out if—and only if—he made a mistake. It wouldn't be staged or done on purpose, but if something went wrong he would let the audience know how he honestly felt.

The night of our show, I talked to the workshop members and gave each a little pep talk and reminders about certain elements of their set. When I got to our friend who had kept us laughing with his fits of frustration, I told him that I hoped he would mess up and not remember parts of his act.

The result was one of the evening's highlights. He started out perfect, forgot his next bit, and threw himself in a mini-rage across a bar stool that was on the stage. At first the audience was shocked (which is a reaction many comedians want), then laughed loudly as he honestly vented his frustrations while continuing to work within his memorized material. It was a wall-pounding, floor-hitting performance that was both unique and funny.

Another way to look at it is to think of the club and audience as a big party. When you're on stage, it's your time to be the host and everyone will want to pay attention to *your* conversation. *You* have something very interesting to tell them, and then do your show as if you wanted to get laughs during a conversation with your party guests.

Don't concern yourself too much with memorization. Good comics constantly change their material and delivery, often depending on what will get the audience laughing harder during that particular show. Always record your act and listen to where the audience laughs and where they don't. You'll probably want to keep the material that worked relatively the same, but make changes to whatever bits might have brought you only blank stares and dead air. When you perform it over and over, you'll find the same laugh lines will be there because you'll want that reaction every time.

Keep in mind where the funny remarks, lines—or whatever it was that stirred your comic interests in the first place—would fit in, and deliver them at that time. How you get there is not important as long as the humor comes through and the laughter is heard.

Now, go outside and repeat to your neighbor everything that was just mentioned. If you don't remember it exactly, just do your best to get the point across. If that fails, try singing "The Brady Bunch Theme Song." I'm sure you'll get a reaction.

Greg Proops

Obviously, stage time is the most important thing. I work it out more on stage. But the "greats," I think, do it more off stage. George Carlin, for instance, will work off stage. He memorizes it before he gets there.

An English comic, Rob Newman, once said to me, "I think rote is a great way to learn." And it's true. If you repeat it a thousand times you'll know it. And then you'll have the freedom to go off of it, add to it, and edit it. I do a lot of that on stage and try to develop it over the course of performing it a bunch of times.

I'll go in with an outline on some things, and some things I want to be real specific about the wording I use, because I tend to use a lot of adjectives and run-on compound sentences. So it's important for me to get the words right. I memorize it over a pattern and then I loosely change things as the mood suits me or the audience. If I get inspired, I'll change something.

You know, I have a joke about Jessica Simpson. "She's a tsunami of stupid. She's a tidal wave of stupid. She's a roller coaster of stupid. She's Six Flags Over Stupid . . ." And it can change each night, the order of it, but there are a couple that are critical to get in the right way.

But I don't think there's any substitute for as much stage time as possible.

FAQ 11 Should I Use a Stage Name?

I took your workshop last year. I was the bitchy redhead, if that helps. I would like to start using a different name when I perform—and I guess that would be a stage name. It's not going to be anything crazy, but I would just like to change my last name. When and how do I do this? Should I use the name I want when sending out videos and photos? Should I introduce myself that way to club owners? Do I have to do something legally in order to use it? Any advice you could give would be appreciated. —M.B.

For cryin' out loud—do you actually think I wouldn't remember a bitchy redhead from one of my workshops? I may not remember what I did yesterday or last week, but I'm usually pretty good at recognizing people with a definite reputation.

Wait a minute . . . does that sound bitchy to you? Well, if people can't remember a name, sometimes an attitude will serve as a reminder. And believe me, there are a lot worse attitudes to deal with than the one you described, except I just can't recall the names of any at the moment. . . .

If you want to use a stage name, make certain this is a definite decision and one you can live with—possibly for a long time. If you're sure, then start using it for all aspects of your comedy career including performances, promotional material, and introductions to club owners. If you go back and forth between two identities, you'll end up confusing bookers who'd like to hire one of you (but maybe not the other), and collecting a lot of business cards from psychiatrists.

When it comes to legal mumbo-jumbo such as signing a contract with a manager or agent, talk to a lawyer about which name to sign. I'm not avoiding any research by suggesting this, because it's always smart to consult a lawyer before ever signing a contract—and you can just throw in that extra question while discussing how much of your life you're actually signing away. Of course, you should check on their "extra questions fee" beforehand, which is made clear in an old joke I found while surfing the Internet:

"How much to you charge?"
"One hundred dollars for three questions," replied the lawyer.
"Isn't that expensive?"
"Yes," he answered. "Now, what's your third question?"

When signing a contract for a single show, you can use your stage name. This is quite common in the industry and should be considered binding for one reason: The person paying you holds all the purse strings. If you default on the show, you won't get paid. There's also a better chance of a lawyer waving his fees than of you ever getting another booking by that person, which is not only a waste of the time and effort you put into it, but also not a smart way to maintain a career. Even if you change your name in an attempt to get a second chance, the possibility always exists that you'll be recognized by your photo or (here we go again) attitude. This time you might be the one cancelled, without the advantage of holding any purse strings.

There's nothing legal that needs to be done when using a stage name. (Example: Carrot Top's real name is Scott Thompson). But if you're looking to use this new persona full-time, then you'll need to deal with lawyers (reread the above example first), and petition the courts for a permanent name change. If that doesn't discourage you, imagine the line at the Department of Motor Vehicles when you go in for that new driver's license.

When you're paid with a check, unless you specify otherwise, chances are the stage name will be on it. I looked into this while managing The Improv in New York City, and the lawyer or accountant (or whoever was charging a fee for my questions) said it was a simple process to cash the check and no legal maneuvering was necessary. Just sign the back of the check with your stage name, then sign your legal name under it. This is similar to a three-party check with you as two-thirds of the parties.

By the way, what's the new name?

Dear Dave,
It's M.C.

Thanks, that helps a lot. At least I'll always remember the attitude.

Earthquake

It [Earthquake] was a childhood name. My real name is Nathaniel Stroman. And when you play for an urban audience, it just don't roll off the tongue. You know, "Give it up for Nathaniel Stroman!" "Boo, nigger! Boo!!" That's right off your name! So I had to get something that would give me a fighting chance.

Weird Al Yankovic

Well, the "Al" part came from my parents. Weird Al is just a nickname I took on when I started doing college radio. I think people were probably calling me Weird Al in the dorms before that! But everybody had some kind of wacky air name like, "Macho Mike" or "Daffy Debbie" or something. So Weird Al seemed appropriate because I played weird music, and it just kind of stuck over the years.

FAQ 12 **Does This Joke Make Me Look Too Old?**

I'm thirteen years old and want to get into comedy. What kind of material should I be thinking about doing? —C.W.

I'm impressed. The only "material" I ever came up with at that age were excuses for why my room was a mess and my homework wasn't done and reasons why everyone seemed to have a girlfriend except me. Since it didn't make teachers, parents, or girls laugh, I never thought about taking it to a comedy stage.

A person your age has a whole wealth of information, experience, and true feelings about being thirteen that more mature (and I use that term loosely) comics don't have anymore. Plus it would be a hard sell for those with an obvious age difference to stand in front of an audience and regress in a believable manner; unless they were playing a childlike character. Talented comedians such as Howie Mandel, Gilda Radner, Lily Tomlin, Jerry Lewis, and others have done this very successfully, but they're still doing characters. Half the fun is realizing they're adults playing off memories, observations, or imagination.

It's always good advice for comedians to talk about what they know. It would be tough to do political commentary if you haven't watched the news or read a newspaper in the past decade. In the same way, I doubt the average teenager would have too much insight on parenthood, divorce, or retirement funds.

In one of my workshops we had a thirteen year old who wanted to do an act similar to Richard Pryor's. I'm sure Child Services will agree when I say that Pryor's style of material is a little too "adult" for someone that age. Pryor has had life experiences and observations that can only come with time, but a thirteen year old is having personal experiences *right now* that anyone more than a few years past their teens can only remember, observe, or make up. Since you are currently living the thirteen-year-old experience, using this firsthand material would make it a unique performance—especially since there aren't many comedians who are your age who share this knowledge.

Most of my writing suggestions are based on being aware of your thoughts and what is going on around you. Many teenagers are thrust into adult situations and lifestyles, which could be very difficult for most audiences to accept or understand. You have to remember that many comedy clubs serve alcohol, and patrons legally have to be over the age of twenty-one. A thirteen year old doing an X-rated act might be hard for them to accept, but a performance kept within (and I hate to say it but, "restricted by") an adult viewpoint of that age group could almost be (and I hate to say this too) endearing. There's a reason why W.C. Fields advised never to work with child actors . . . they can always steal the scene.

Also keep in mind that your source of material, writing, and performance skills will be growing with you. This should continue giving you a lot of comedy ideas in the next few years because most of your audiences should remember being teenagers (except for those who still find the 1960s a little blurry), and you can get them laughing with insights on what it's like now.

Bobcat Goldthwait

I started doing stand-up when I was like sixteen years old in Syracuse, but I moved to Boston when I was eighteen and did it full time there. Then I got on Letterman when I was twenty.

I never really did traditional stand-up. When I first started out I would gut fish on stage or read a Dear John letter. I just did more kind of conceptual stuff. I just felt it would be much harder for me to go out and talk about, you know, driving or something. Then, over the years, I became a comic. But it's not like I do something completely different than who I am. By the time you get on stage, it's a scary place. So you've already got adrenaline running; I just use that. I've always used that as my catalyst on stage.

I could never see not doing stand-up. It's what I've been doing since I was sixteen and even in the eighties when I had a lot of heat, I still always went out and did stand-up while I was making movies.

FAQ 13 What Should I Do When I'm Not Feeling Funny?

Sometimes I just don't feel like performing. I'm in a bad mood because something's gone wrong or it might have been a bad day. I'm not up to giving it my best, but I hate to cancel a spot I've worked so hard to get. —J.J.

Comedians are not wind-up toys that can be started and stopped on a whim. They're human beings with emotions. Moods, exhaustion, physical ailments, or even a bad run at the crap table can make performing more work than fun, but those most dedicated find a way to get through it.

Depending on how you feel is a real factor, but you can't let it take away from your performance. If you're mad or depressed, maybe you'll find that night's "edge" makes your act funnier. If so, you learned something—which is to keep it in the act! If it doesn't, then do your best to block out your problems while you're on stage.

I know that sounds easier said than done, but it's an element of the business that you'll most likely have to deal with someday. For example, a comedian I booked for *A&E's An Evening At The Improv* had to cancel his spot, the afternoon of the taping. I needed a replacement who also needed to be funny—and I needed him right away. So I called Bobby Collins, who at the time was living near where we did the taping. He was sick and in bed with a high fever, but it wasn't enough to keep him from adding another television credit to his résumé. He walked to the club right before he was scheduled to appear, did a seven-minute set like he was the healthiest person on earth, then dragged himself home and back to his sick bed. We still laugh that he must have sweated off ten pounds that night, but he lived up to the old showbiz adage, "The show must go on."

Another comedian I worked with was going through a bad breakup with his girlfriend. He was "this close" to crying real tears one night at the New York Improv when he was announced as the next performer. He let out a big laugh (as he always did), ran onto the stage, and performed his usual hysterical set. When he finished, he walked to the back of the club, and the first thing he asked me was if his girlfriend had called. Yes, the show must go on, even though your heart and mind want to be somewhere else.

There undoubtedly will be times when you simply won't be able to perform. We're all human and it's part of the price we pay to play the game of life. When you're too sick, hurt, or emotional to get on stage, it's not the end of the world (unless you have a doctor's note saying it is). You need a break to heal yourself and be ready to take advantage of the next opportunity your hard work will bring. Bookers may sound grumpy when you cancel, but the professional ones are very aware that a legitimate excuse is part of the business. When you give them enough time to find a substitute performer (better still, suggest one you know is available to make their life easier), they shouldn't hold it against you. If they do, then you probably wouldn't enjoy working for them anyway.

When comedy is your career, you need to treat it that way and dedicate yourself to it. There are people with *normal* jobs who might also be having a bad day because something went wrong. But unless they feel it's worth sacrificing a sick day or vacation time, they have to go to work. Besides, a comedian has the energy of a live audience to either help them cheer up or on which to take out their frustrations. In my opinion, it's probably more difficult to do that while sitting behind a desk, fighting fires, or directing traffic for eight hours a day.

These aren't examples to write home about, but I think you get the idea. Do your best to take advantage of your hard work and be ready every time you walk on stage. If how you're feeling helps the show, then use it. If not, check those feelings at the club entrance and pick them up on the way out.

Bobby Collins

What we do doesn't make for who we are as human beings. I'm a comedian, but I'm also a husband, father, and a businessman in my office. I wear different hats.

The hat that comes most natural and easy for me is the art of performing. So I know if other parts of my life get me down—I'm having a fight with the wife, one of the kids is sick, or I'm sick—I know performing is the passion in my heart that makes me feel better about all those other hats I wear. It's what makes me feel the best and why those other things exist. It's because of the thing I do the best—and that is to stand on a stage.

So the passion I have for stand-up and the passion I have for the stage . . . It's like I love two women in my life. My wife Jill, who I love. But that stage is a lady in itself and when I stand on it, boy, do I respect it. And I pay homage to it. Thank you. You not only made my living—you are the thing that makes me feel the best about who I am in my heart. I'm the most comfortable performing. I'm very comfortable up there.

When I'm sick, man, I know that I need to sweat. And instead of going out and running because I'm too weak, I'll get up and perform. And it makes everything just

Making Conversation

- **Day Job.** What you do for a living while waiting to become a successful comedian. It doesn't matter if you are a corporate banker or you wash pans (and I've done one of those, but won't tell which). The term is a reference made toward how you make money during normal hours, as opposed to the abnormal hours spent in comedy clubs trying to stay awake because of this financial necessity.

- **Trade Papers.** Newspapers or magazines geared toward the entertainment industry. Some of the better known are *Back Stage, Showbusiness, Variety, The Hollywood Reporter,* and *Billboard.* They often include reports about the business aspects, performance reviews, upcoming shows or events, interviews, financial reports, and, most importantly for performers, audition notices. True, the acting community might find these more valuable, but some publish special comedy issues or list open mike opportunities. Larger cities also have weekly newspapers that dedicate sections to entertainment such as New York's *Village Voice* and *LA Weekly* in Los Angeles that will tell you when, where, and how to get on stage.

- **The Comedy Boom.** Members of the comedy industry look back at the years between the mid-eighties and early nineties as a time when comedy exploded in popularity. Comics such as Bill Cosby, Roseanne, Jerry Seinfeld, Brett Butler, and Tim Allen had hit television silcoms, and casting directors were constantly scouting clubs looking for new talent. Network and cable television schedules were filled with stand-up comedy shows that included *A&E's An Evening At The Improv, Caroline's Comedy Hour, Comic Strip Live, MTV's Half Hour Comedy Hour, The A-List, VH-1's Stand-Up Spotlight,* and many others. Every city seemed to have a number of comedy clubs while smaller towns were turning bars, bowling alleys, diners, and almost any type of location into a cover charge and drink minimum gold mine. To make a long story short, there was a lot of work available for comics. Another name for this would be "The Good Old Days."

feel so much better. It just makes me feel physically better, mentally better, and more alert. So I would just probably rustle myself out and go out and get up on a stage, rather than lie home and feel sorry for myself. But that's what I do.

It is a job sometimes. But sometimes you can turn a situation around. You could be having a really bad day and things aren't going well and the connections aren't connecting and you're not feeling good. You lost two jobs, you came in second at some hot comedy contest, and you didn't get that Las Vegas gig, or something else in the business world. But I know that by me getting up on that stage, that's what makes me feel good. All that other stuff becomes secondary. What's prime is the fact that I'm a performer. And if you love it—you do it.

Part Two ON STAGE

 ON STAGE

I'm still trying to figure out "who I am" on stage. I know I can't be someone I'm not, but there are certain comics I really enjoy and consider my influences. I would never steal their material or copy them, but they make me laugh the same way I want to make audiences laugh. I'm pretty high-energy and those are the types of comics that got me interested in doing this in the first place. How much should I let other comics influence me? —T.R.

Unless you're living in a shack in a woods (which is different from a van by the river) without electricity or any contact with the outside world, you're going to be influenced by someone or something. Since I can't think of any Uni-Comics populating wooded areas and creating jokes from nature, it's a safe bet watching someone who was already doing it inspired the ones you see in clubs and on television.

Comedians are not isolated people. They don't just walk out of the woods one day with a brilliant idea to go on stage and make people laugh. They were inspired or influenced by seeing a comedian on television, on stage, or hearing a recording. You can't escape it. If your friends keep saying you're funny and should be a comedian, you know exactly what they're talking about.

If someone (a comedian), or something (a pie in the face), makes you laugh, it's an example of the type of humor you enjoy. When you're putting together an act, you're not going to perform anything you don't think is funny—are you? Of course not. Your sense of humor influences what you say and do on stage.

When you ask comedians who their influences are, they'll usually have a few answers. Lenny Bruce and George Carlin opened the doors for comedians to question authority. Bill Cosby showed it was funny to tell stories about family and life experiences. Richard Pryor brought reality to the stage, and Jerry Seinfeld is an observer of real life as he sees it.

Politics, family, reality, and observational comedy. Do they sound like unique topics? Not really. Quite a few comedians cover those subjects, but the key is to have unique thoughts and an individual persona on stage. You're correct in saying you'd never steal or copy from someone else. That's the kiss of death for any performer—and a way to show they've influenced you too much.

Influenced—yes. Copycat—no.

Comedians have different opinions on how much you should watch other performers. Some will say to watch as much comedy as possible so you have an idea of what is successful in clubs and on television. Others will claim they never watch comics because they don't want to be influenced. The choice is yours, but never lose sight of who *you* are.

In fact, you might even be influenced to go in a completely different direction. I once had the opportunity to talk with Rita Rudner about her comedy beginnings. There was an open mike in New York City that we both knew and had often attended. Rita said she'd watch the other acts and make mental notes *never* to do anything remotely similar to what they did on stage. The end result made her one of the most unique comedians in the business.

Margaret Cho

I really think the most interesting comedy is when you learn more about the comedian. Like when you learn more about what they think about things that happened. When they're able to take things that are painful in their life and make them funny and share them. They share that journey with the audience and relate it successfully. I think that's extraordinary and I just admire that.

I really miss Bill Hicks. I feel like that's what I want to be. To be really good like that. He was so good and so nice, but once he got on stage he didn't give a shit. And just the way that he had such an incredible gift of detail and a gift of describing things so perfectly. And the gift of metaphor and all these different things. Such an incredible grasp of language and a love of it, which is kind of rare in comedy because now it's so easy to fall into these traps of being one thing and not exploring or not taking chances. He was the master at taking risks, and I try to emulate that always on stage. I don't know if I ever will attain what he had and I don't mean to even believe that I could, but every time I step on stage I feel as if it's almost an homage to him.

I saw George Carlin do a [television] special in Aspen. I was so inspired because as a comic, I think you can get depressed sometimes because the road seems so endless and hard. You think, "Where's this going?" And then you look at Carlin and you think, "Ah, that's where it goes!" He made me feel so good about the whole thing.

George Carlin

What it did was remind her of her own goal. Reminded her of her own destination. I'm happy in that instance that I was the one who did that. You know, that it was seeing me that brought that out. But she had all that going for her anyway and she could've noticed that from someone else. You know?

Who's Who When the Spotlight Is On

- **The MC.** Also known as the opening act, host, master of ceremonies, and emcee. This is normally the first person on stage during a show. Sometimes the owner or manager of a club will go on stage to introduce the MC, but the label goes to the first performer of the evening who will then introduce the following acts.

- **The Feature Act.** Also known as the middle act. In a three-comedian show, which is a format many clubs outside of New York City and Los Angeles adhere to, this is the second performer. He generally will have more on-stage time than the MC, but not as much as the headliner.

- **The Headliner.** This is the final and "star" performer. The headlining comedian is the climax of the show and who the club owner is banking on to fill seats with paying customers. He's expected to keep an audience laughing for a full forty-five minutes to an hour—or risk being invited back next time as a feature act.

But a lot of people have told me that, "I'm only doing this because of you, because I heard your records," or this and that and everything. And those are nice things because when you get visible and you are heard and known . . .

It's just like writers have a kind of an influence they don't know about. It could be from all over the world or all through their lives in the years that passed. It's just the way the human community works. We all build on the ideas and inspiration of others and try to make our own dreams come true.

Dom Irrera

When people ask me, "How do you headline?" I go, "Well, you don't headline. They make you headline." You have to be so good that no middle and no closing act wants to follow you. And customers are going up to the owner of the club and going, "You gotta get this guy here to do the long spot." You know? That's how you headline.

There's no magic formula. But it's hard work, you know? And it takes talent. Of course it takes luck, but the one thing good about stand-up is when you're so good and audiences like you so much, nobody can deny that. Maybe you won't get a series because you're not Aaron Spelling's daughter, but at least you'll work. If you're good enough. Now I can get off my high horse and start talking about my own miserable career. . . .

Dennis Regan

When I'm a middle act, I don't like to be brought up as "the feature," because it can be confusing to the audience. When you go to the movies and it says, "Feature Presentation," it's the main thing. You don't want the audience going, "Where's the [advertised] headliner?"

Comics don't understand. They think because they know something so well that the audience knows it. I think in Ireland and maybe throughout England, they call the headliner "the main act." And what we call the feature, the middle act, they call "the support act." I like those terms better than ours. Especially the support act.

One of the things about going up as a middle is that the dynamic is a lot different. A lot of people don't realize that. When you go up as a middle, the audience expectation and their attitude is a lot different. If they don't like you right off the bat, they're still okay because you're just the middle. They're more forgiving or they come along because they know the headliner is coming on later. When you go up as a headliner and they don't like you within the first five minutes, it's a different dynamic. You might have to follow somebody that they loved and now they're looking at you like, "What? You're gonna do forty-five minutes?" You really have to know how to pull out of that.

You need a lot of confidence. You have to be reassuring to them that it's going to be okay. I especially have a hard time with it sometimes because I'm low energy. I'll get to a place where they'll have a guitar player because they want a balanced show with a high-energy act. Or it might be someone who's really dirty. So when you get up there, you just have to muscle through. I do my act. I might make some adjustments and front-load some easier things, but my point here is that it's quite a different dynamic going up as the closing act. That's part of the reason I don't like to be brought up as the "feature act." I don't want that kind of pressure, if I'm not getting that kind of money!

When people are middling and they've got thirty minutes of material, they might think they're fifteen minutes away from headlining. It's a lot further away than that. You've got to have a lot more material than that and a lot more stage savvy.

FAQ 15 **How Long Can I Stick to the Same Old Routine?**

Regarding the contents of your act, how long can you show up at every open-mike night in the same club and do the same routine? In other words, how long can you play a ten- to twelve-minute set in one place before writing new material? I realize it's probably a different audience each week, but at some point the organizers of the show are going to get tired of hearing the same stuff. —J.W.

I've often wondered about this dilemma myself. I deliver the same routine to my kids every week: "Clean your room, mow the lawn, and don't bother your father when he's sleeping." I know they get tired of hearing it, but I keep repeating myself because they act like an audience hearing it for the first time.

People in the comedy industry know how difficult it can be to write good material. If you have the talent to sit down at a keyboard and effortlessly compose a great seven-minute *Tonight Show* quality set, then consider joining the few others who can and start earning a lot of money in Hollywood as a writer.

If the person running the open mike is new to the comedy business, it might help your comfort level to explain why you are doing the same routine each time. Let him know you are working to hone your act and make it more professional. It's a good use of stage time and something all comedians must do to make the act better.

I once saw a very famous comedian who was on tour and only performing in large theaters. Since his star-power would cause too much of a commotion if he appeared at local open-mike rooms, he announced to the audience that he was in the process of putting together new material for a cable television special. He was working out the kinks by doing the same routine every night because it *had* to be funny and practiced. You're doing the same thing.

To show some diversity, you might want to change the order of your material. This is also good practice to break any reliance you might have about memorizing a set. Depending on the audience and what types of jokes are working better that night, good comedians have learned how to edit their material on the spot. Or better yet—in the spotlight. It's a technique you should start perfecting now.

To continue growing as a comedian, chances are you'll eventually feel stifled doing the exact same material every night. Make an effort to work in something new at each open mike, even if it's only one joke or bit. Unless you're practicing for a specific audition where you want your showcase to be as "killer" as possible, use open-mike clubs to get better while still developing new material. This will show people who see you on a regular basis that you're continuing to work on your craft.

You might also want to spend a few minutes talking and working off the audience. This technique may not be part of how you envision yourself as a comedian, but it will add diversity to your act. Keep in mind that just about every comedian will have to do this at one point or another because the first paying jobs are usually as an MC. The main duties of an MC are . . . well, I'll cover that in a moment because right now my kids are waiting to hear my daily routine.

Richard Jeni

Eventually people will get tired of hearing the stuff. They can hear it more than once, oddly enough. I mean, people will come to shows and because they've seen certain things on TV, they want to hear them in a live situation, you know? It's like having it on television sort of glamorizes it. And when they come to see you in a live situa-tion, it feels like it has that, "as seen on TV" aspect. It's like, "Wow, that was seen on TV in front of millions of people, and now here it is just for us!" But eventually they'll tire of it. I mean, you can do it once, twice, three times . . . whatever. But at some point, people are gonna go, "We've seen this guy." You know? If you keep doing the same stuff . . . "We love him, he's great. But we've seen it!" And how many times can you see it? So partially, why I keep coming up with the stuff, is just for survival.

The other reason . . . You know these people that do stage plays for, like, ten years? You know, the guy . . . What was that play . . .? Oh yeah, he was in My Fair Lady *for ten years. About the thirtieth time that I had to go, "The rain in Spain . . ." I'd take out a bazooka and blow my brains out! The only thing that keeps it interesting to me, that keeps it on the edge, is writing new stuff and trying new stuff. Wondering if it's gonna work, honing it and fixing it, and being elated when it does and depressed when it doesn't. That's what keeps me on the edge and keeps me wanting to do it. If I just sort of "got" my act and went, "Okay, this is a really funny hour of stuff and I'll just keep doing it until I drop dead," I would be bored. That would start to feel like a job.*

The first time I did an HBO special I thought, "Well, okay, I can never do this material again." But then people would get pissed if you didn't do it. At least some of it. Because they do feel like they, you know, told their friend in the car that he's gonna do this thing about . . . "Wait 'til you see him do the football thing!" And if you don't do it, it kinda makes them look bad. This show I do now is sort of a combination of quote/unquote "Greatest Hits," with a lot of new material sprinkled in.

FAQ 16 What's Expected of a Good MC?

I compromised my amateur status by taking gas money this weekend. I was supposed to do an unpaid guest spot at a club Friday night, but the MC cancelled and they told me I had the job. Thank God I had more than the five minutes I was planning to do! After my set the club manager told me to plan on MCing Saturday and that he'd give me $20 if I promised not to mention it to anyone (the club owner, other comics, and the IRS). So finally, someone paid me to make an audience laugh!

It was a big step up for me. The talent level of the other comedians was considerably better than what I'm used to working with. It reminded me of how far I need to go to get to that level. I guess that's a good thing. The club manager told me I did well and he gave the agency a good report. They called yesterday to rebook me! The other comics said it was nice to work with a new comic who had material, got their names right, did the obligatory announcements, and respected what they were doing. All in all, I guess it was a good weekend. —E.C.

Yeah, I'd call it a good weekend, too, if someone gave me twenty bucks and I didn't have to mention it to my wife (let alone the IRS). But I think chances are in your favor that you'll have a lot more MC work before I can start a secret money stash.

Whether you're getting paid or only working for stage time, it's important to keep in mind the job description for a good MC. And keeping in line with almost everything else in the comedy business, you'll learn through experience that there will be exceptions. Much of this will come through trial and error while on stage, or as many seasoned MC's will warn you—trial by fire. It's always a good idea to talk to the manager of the club and find out what they expect from their MCs, but if you want to make a good first impression, here are a few tips on how to correctly get the job done:

1. The MC must welcome the audience and make it clear they picked the right place for entertainment. Tell them they're about to see a great show and try to interact while making your guests feel comfortable. This is an excellent opportunity to work on valuable improvisational skills. Be original ("Where'd you get that shirt?!") or ask a few audience members the basic comedy questions ("Where are you from?" and "What do you do

for a living?"). Then play off their response. Let the crowd know the show has started as soon as you hit the stage.

2. Club owners will expect you to make all the required announcements. For instance: the drink and food specials, headliners appearing in the future, discounts available for groups or parties, sponsors that provided transportation and hotel rooms, radio stations that feature the club's acts on the air, why this club is the best club in the universe, and a reminder to tip the wait staff. Experienced MCs can make these announcements very clear to everyone in the room, while delivering what are essentially advertisements in a way—that integrates them into their comedy routine. For instance: *"If you buy one of the club's shirts and wear it on Tuesday nights, you get in free. If you wear one every night, they might make you the opening act. That's what I did!"*

   It's important to have fun while never actually insulting the club or the sponsors—or at least make it clear you're only joking. If you also make the audience laugh, you'll be doing a good job.

3. Introduce the other performers. Some comedians have a regular intro-duction they'll want you to give or a detailed list of their credits. Others may choose to keep it simple, such as: "Plays clubs and colleges across the country, let's have a big hand for . . ." It's not a crime to write the requested introduction on a piece of paper and use it on stage. In fact, you might find a valuable comedy ally by making an effort to get the headliner's introduction exactly the way they want it.

4. If you have any time after that, being funny is a good option.

The amount of time an MC has on stage depends on the format of the show. When three acts are involved (along with the feature and headliner), the MC will have the least amount of time to perform.

The club manager will tell an MC how much time she is expected to do when opening the show. But if the manager doesn't, then it's wise to ask. If it's a typical weeknight with only one performance, the time can range from five to seven minutes or up to as much as twenty. The MC might also be able to do a few minutes between the feature and headline acts.

If it's a weekend with two or three shows the same night, then a tighter schedule must be used to keep the starting time of the following shows close to what is advertised. During the earlier performances, there is normally less stage time available. Because the audience is supposedly there to see the headliner, his amount of time on stage will be kept relatively the same. And since the feature act has earned a higher slot in the show, you can bet your twenty bucks that if any time is going to be cut, it'll come from the opening act.

This means the MC should follow steps one through three listed above. If there's any time for the fourth step, make the most of it.

On these occasions, the final show is usually more relaxed. There's not a set time it has to end, unless there's a curfew or the manager has a hot date. Normally the MC will be given an opportunity to do his act.

In a showcase club, mostly in New York or Los Angeles, there will be more comedians on the schedule doing shorter sets. On some nights there can be as many as fourteen or fifteen, and sometimes more. In these cases, the MC has a much bigger role. He is expected to warm-up the audience so they're ready to laugh. This could mean starting out with a ten to fifteen minute set, then introducing the acts when it's their turn. If a comedian has a great set, the MC would keep the show rolling by wasting little time in bringing up the next performer. If the comic doesn't get the desired amount of laughs, the MC might do another short set to get the audience back on track. During the course of the evening, the MC can make the necessary announcements and perform material.

If the MC spot means opening the show in a theater for a star attraction, the stakes are higher and a proven routine is a must. Quite often this type of prestigious booking will go to a comedian who is already a headliner or feature on the club circuit. They could be required to perform twenty to thirty minutes of audience-tested material to give a big event a grand opening while warming-up the crowd for the act they actually paid a higher ticket price to see. It would be difficult for an open-mike performer to get his first MC spot opening for Cher in Las Vegas or The Kings of Comedy in a sold-out auditorium. But once you reach that level there should be more than $20 to worry about keeping secret.

Dave Attell

I'm not a very good MC. I tried it a couple of times and I was never good at it. A good MC is a guy who realizes the show is not about him. That he's got a lot of bitter pricks waiting to get on and that him doing an hour and a half in

between acts does not help the show. It might help him, but it doesn't help the show. So the MCs are people who make it a show. You know, they're the glue. It's an important job.

Wendy Liebman

Sometimes performing is more work than other times. Like the audience isn't completely there or I'm not completely on. But I guess one of my harder shows was when I worked a couple of years ago for Nike. They hired me for a corporate party, and the show was on a basketball court. People were playing basketball in the background and there were

about four sofas set up. I was on a platform that was, like, twenty feet above them. And there was no momentum. You know how laughter is contagious? And people laugh harder when they're anonymous. It's better if the audience is huge and in the dark.

So here I am performing for twelve people sitting on couches, and other people are playing basketball. Nike had flown me in and given me all this Nike stuff and treated me first class. And I'm sitting there going, "Okay, well, I'll take their advice and Just Do It!" It really was an impossible situation, but I Just Did It. In my contract rider, now, it says there cannot be a basketball game going on in the same venue.

FAQ 17   What Do I Do if I Am Just Not Connecting with the Audience?

I'm finding on the open-mike circuit that different material works on different audiences. So I can't always rely on the audience to tell me what's funny and what's not. I know I've got to learn to size up the audience to find out what material might be a better fit, so I mix up my routine. This is often based on what bits I know have worked in the past, ones I need to work on, or trying out new material. But if I get different reactions to the same stuff, it's tough to figure out what's working for real. At some shows they laugh all the way through, but other times they just sit there and stare at me. Any suggestions? —J.J.

You pretty much answered your own question with the first sentence. If the audience is laughing, they're telling you the material is working—at least for them. When they're not, then you're being told you need to give that "tough crowd" something they will laugh at. Audience reaction will always tell you what is and what isn't working in each situation.

A comic must learn to read his audience. This can be easy or difficult and depends on the venue as much as the people waiting to be entertained. Some acts can get laughs anywhere, and others might do better in New York City than in Oklahoma City. Every audience has its own personality. A good comedian will find out what it is and find a way for them to relate to his material.

With that said, the best advice in any situation is to stay true to yourself as a comedian. You've worked hard on your material and stage persona, and should never discard it entirely just to please one audience. If you're consistently not getting laughs, it could be an indication that a drastic change might be in order (like a new act). Otherwise, learn to make a few adjustments for different crowds.

If an act that has been successful in the past is suddenly not working, try to personalize it more for the audience. Making slight changes in your delivery or the material can do this. You may have to be more aggressive in certain situations, or more laid-back. You could even change some of the references to include the area where you're performing and the crowd's awareness of the topics, making it more "real" for them.

For example, you might talk about riding in a New York City taxi as something you do almost every day. There's a good chance most audience members in Oklahoma City have never been in a NYC cab. Instead of delivering the bit as if it were second nature, give them more of a description and help them visualize this very different experience. The opposite is also true. New York City audiences are probably not familiar with everything that goes on in Oklahoma. If that's your subject, explain it as you would to any other first-time visitor.

Some topics will just not work for certain audiences. Grandparents can be very different than teenagers. If your material is geared for one and not the other, you either find a way to help them relate on a personal level or make a conscious effort to play either senior events or senior prom shows—and not both.

It's also true that simple changes in language or sexual content will affect audiences in different ways. It's a general assumption patrons at a midnight show or sleazy bar will expect material that's a bit more risqué than what was performed during an early evening show. With that in mind, some comics adjust their material accordingly.

Using this risqué technique depends on the personal choices you've made as a comedian. As mentioned above, stay true to yourself. If it goes against everything you're working to achieve by using four-letter words or graphic sex jokes, don't give in. You may have to avoid accepting these types of shows, but eventually you'll find your audience.

If you have no problem getting down and dirty—or cleaning it up, if it's an early show with grandparents and teens—then go for the laughs. None of us reading this book invented the motto, "Give the audience what they want," so in certain cases it can be good advice. It's your decision.

Another technique in trying to relate to an audience is by asking if anyone has had a similar experience or any thoughts on a subject. Your attitude during a performance can make a difference. If your material is about children, ask if anyone has children and deliver your material in a way that would include the audience members you're talking to. Be more of a friend than a performer. Verbally play with the crowd to learn what type of humor they might have in common as a group. If they laugh, you've made the necessary adjustments. If not, just do your act and consider it a learning experience. Try to be your best every time you walk on stage. If your act is not working, attempt to bring the audience into the material on a more personal level. Remember, each audience is like a different person and you have to treat them that way.

George Carlin

When things don't go well, it's always the audience's fault. It has to be. Because if you believe in the stuff and it's worked a sufficient number of times on stage for you to keep doing it or to be trying it that night, the fact that they're not all there with it is their fault. There's nothing you can do about that.

The problem with getting started in comedy when you don't have a name or a reputation is that you really don't know who you are. This is not true of guys who begin to get a little club recognition. People who come to clubs and see a mid-level comic or someone who has established an identity in the minds of the audience already have something going for them. Even they can have a bad night and they're certainly not worried about changing the material.

The problem with being brand new is that it's all a guessing game on your part. In stand-up comedy, you never have a finished product when you're starting out. You go out for two nights, five nights, twenty nights, and every time you come home you're starting to rewrite things based on what you heard that night. Over time, certain things get established. But it's always this guessing game because you can't predict them—and they can't predict you. Then you have to meet the laws of probability. Some nights you'll just get a higher percentage of people who aren't very outgoing, demonstrative, responsive, or energetic. Or they're not very smart or don't want to be there, but they're with people who brought them. There are all kinds of things you can't account for that are in the stars.

If I've got a theater full of twenty-two hundred people, the ones that don't quite fit aren't noticed. But in an audience of one hundred, twenty people who aren't with it can affect the people around them. There's just very little you can do except have faith in the material because it worked before.

When I used to bomb at the Cafe au Go Go in my first few years as a single, and I'd be riding home on the subway, I would say to myself, "It's their fault, because Friday night was great. And Friday night has to be the one that counts. Not tonight. Tonight is not the norm."

The problem with open mikes is you only get three minutes or eight minutes, whatever it is. Half the audiences are jaded comics, or jaded agents or managers out hustling talent; they're not high on the scale. So you've got a lot of obstacles to fight with open mikes.

Dennis Regan

How to deal with people that are not laughing? First of all, do nothing! Leave them alone! It's unrealistic to think that everyone is going to like your act. Even when you are killing, it's not hard to find someone who's just not into it. They have a right not to be into it, so just leave them alone and be glad they're not screwing with you. I've seen too many comics go after a guy in the front row just because he wasn't laughing.

Having said that, one time I was doing a show in Hilton Head, South Carolina. Small crowd of about twenty people—mostly couples on vacation. I did about as well as you could do in that circumstance and did about an hour. But for most of the time there was this woman stage left that had her head on her husband's shoulder. It bugged me some, but I told myself—hey, who knows what her deal is. She could be tired, sunburned, or might not speak English very well. But it continued to bug me, even though I could not have been happier with the rest of the crowd and the way the set was going.

After the set, I was having a beer at the little bar in the back of the room. Most of the crowd had left, but some stragglers were using the bathroom, etc. . . . . The woman came up to me and said, "I just want you to know that I think what you do is very important and I think you are great at it."

I thanked her and then said, "I couldn't help but notice that you had your head on your husband's shoulder most of the time. I thought you were bored."

She said, "Oh no! I'm deaf and I was able to read your lips better from that angle." She went on to tell me that for most of her life she had been a workaholic and then five years before at the age of forty, was diagnosed with a brain tumor. It had since been removed, but she lost her hearing in the process. She stated that she felt fine, but that her future was uncertain. She said that her outlook was completely

different and that all she wanted to do was laugh. Then she repeated her initial state-
ment to me about what I was doing being very important. And, oh yeah, about me
being great at it!

When someone isn't laughing, leave them alone. You just don't know what their
situation is.

FAQ 18 Should I Be Mr. Clean or The Dirt Devil?

Is it better to work dirty or clean? I'm not out to shock audiences, but I like
the X-rated stuff better than watching what I say all the time. I think it's
@#$'ing funny! —J.K.*

I'm in the same situation with your question. I have to watch what I say
because this debate can get @#$*'ing ugly. Both sides are always right when
there's laughter—or wrong when there's not.

When walking this fine line between clean and dirty, only one thing is
certain. The type of show will dictate the rating of your material. If you
want to work the corporate, college, cruise ship markets or network
television, Mr. Clean is the most employable. That's a fact you can take to
the cleaners.

Comedy clubs, concerts, and cable television can go either way.
It depends on the audience and any rules management has for performance
content.

The reality is that both sides have an audience. The Dirt Devil can fill
venues with X-rated material and paying customers, but so can Mr. Clean. The
common ground is laughter.

You need to make your own decision on this one. If you love performing
X-rated material and it works with audiences, that's your style. The opposite
is also true. Be honest with yourself and your talent. If you're uncomfortable
with either direction, the audience will sense it. They won't laugh and you
won't be employed—at least in the comedy industry.

Many experienced comedians can work both sides of this debate. They want
the paycheck that comes from performing clean at corporate functions, while
also filling every seat at a midnight "anything goes" show at a club. Their goal
could be having both a cable television special with no restrictions and appearances on network television during family hours. A way to do it is by preparing
different material or having the option to change what you already have.

A good idea—if you want to play both sides—is not to let your punch lines depend on an X-rating. These words or descriptions can be included or deleted depending on the audience and venue. Have the ability to be Mr. Clean or The Dirt Devil whenever it works to your benefit.

Of course I'm still walking that thin line and can be easily pushed off-balance by dedicated supporters of either side. When it comes to the clean versus dirty debate, there is no wrong when everybody's right. You need to do what you're good at and comfortable with, decide what markets you want to be successful in—then work to be the @#$*'ing best at it.

Flex Alexander

The thing I'm most excited about is that [I do] a clean show. It's fun, but because people hear, "clean show," they go, "Oh no, it's gonna be soft!" Hey, it's still a great show. It doesn't have to be, "Yeah, so I stuck this in her butt! Thank you! Good night!" You know? I think, for the most part, it can be a cheap way to make people laugh. There are some people who are whizzes at it, like George Carlin, who I love! He's so smart. But I wanted to do something different to open it up to more people.

I wasn't a clean comic when I started, but I wasn't the filthiest either. I would just watch the reactions of the people. People would come to me and go, "That would be funny if you didn't say, mother-something-something in her butt." You know? I just tried to pay attention to that over the years.

Then I said, "You know what? Let's do something different. Let's open it up." And you watch people like Sinbad, who's had great longevity. And I have a kid now, and it takes on a whole new meaning because I want her to be able to watch me.

I used to sneak up and listen to Richard Pryor's records while I was growing up. And the first time I saw Eddie Murphy's "Delirious" was when I said, "That's what I want to do!" A lot of talented comedians used it [X-rated material], and that's what I grew up on. But I guess to rephrase, it would be "the newer regime" is only looking for the shock value. When they write the joke, they put the curse in there:

"'I'm walking down the street . . . No. I'm walking down the MFing street and . . . Yeah, that's it right there!" And they have material.

George Carlin

It is an individual thing and it does have to do with the tone and sensibility of the comedian's whole act and demeanor. The words should never seem out of place for the individual. They should seem to naturally enhance something this individual is saying.

The media has said this a lot of times—you know, it's a cliché. They say, "Some of these guys seem like they're just using X-rated material for shock value."

And they're right to an extent. There are some comedians who take too much license. Liberty and license are different. I'm not gonna worry about that distinction, because it takes too much thought. But there's a difference between being able to do something, and doing it for no reason. It should enhance. It should be used as a sea-soning would be used in a stew. If you put in too much of any of the seasonings, you spoil the stew. The ingredients of the stew are what's important. The seasonings help underline and enhance.

Is It Just Me, Or Is It Hot In Here?

- **Warm-Up the Audience.** Preparing an audience to laugh at the upcoming acts–by making them laugh. This can be the hardest job to have during a show because the audience is "cold" when they first arrive. In other words, they just finished traveling to the club, paid parking, paid admission, were given a table not exactly where they wanted to be, almost fainted at the food and drink prices, found the people next to them annoying, and have the attitude that the first person on stage better be funny–or else. The first comedian needs to break this ice so the following performers get a warmer reception.

- **A Hack.** A reference toward a comedian who uses old jokes, tired clichés, worn-out subjects, or juvenile bathroom humor that should have been flushed out of a respectable act after only a few open mikes. The only thing worse is to be called a thief for using another comic's material.

- **On The Edge.** In other words, the comic is "out there." This means his material can be considered risky, controversial, or not politically correct. There's a good chance he might offend part of the audience while taking the rest to new heights of comedy hysterics. It's similar to getting in a roller coaster without a safety bar. If you make it, you're a legend. If not, you crash and burn.

I also do some flat-out raunchy lines, which are supposed to be raunchy. I'll come out and I'll say, "Something people don't talk about in public anymore. Pussy farts." Well, that's just to wake 'em up. There are things that I say that you could say have no redeeming, social artistic value. But I have long stretches in my act when there are no curses at all. And an occasional "fuck" in one of those really stands out and does the job.

If the landscape is flat and suddenly there's a mountain or a hill or a butte or a mesa, it really stands out. It means something. If the landscape is all mesas and mountains and buttes and so forth, then they don't mean anything. They all kind of run together.

So it has to be used so that it stands out as doing a job. It has to get a job done for you. To throw them around is just to waste money. It's a form of currency and you don't spend it extravagantly. You should be thrifty and use them where they help and where it is obvious to the audience that you don't need those things. You're not depending on that to take the place of being smart, clever, funny, and intelligent.

Lisa Lampanelli

I've never made a conscious effort to be dirty or clean onstage. The only thing I consciously decided was to be one hundred percent myself. What I mean is that, if you talk to me in real life, I curse and I say crazy ethnic things. So, why would I be any different onstage?

Now, how could I expect an audience to love me if I'm not being myself onstage? If I'm holding back and being squeaky clean and politically correct, I'm not being Lisa

Lampanelli. If I were to do that, audience members would hold back too and not be the devoted, rabid fans they would be if I was being myself. Of course, not compromising on stage has closed some doors to me like the Lettermans and the Lenos and things like that. But I think it has and will continue to open other doors for me. Doors like Howard Stern, other morning radio people, and more politically incorrect TV programs like BET Comic View *and the* Friars Club Roasts.

Most importantly, wherever I am, I'm creating these insane fans who want to come back again and again and who say, "Oh my God—we just love you!" I always said, "I don't want them to like me. I want them to love me." And you only love about 5 percent of the comics out there. I think that's because that 5 percent are who they are, and they don't edit. And me not editing is what makes people love me. It may not get me on every show, but it's getting me on the right shows for me.

Thank God, it's been working so far. And it's funny because this philosophy works in real life too. Did you ever notice that when you were on a date and you were 100 percent yourself, the relationship ended up happening? Don't hold back ever and the right people—managers, agents, audience members, men, women—will be attracted to you! In real life and in comedy, it just works.

FAQ 19   What About . . . Pauses during Your Delivery?

Any comments on how to learn where they [pauses] need to be, or is it just trial and error to see what works? —T.M.

Imagine asking the late, great Jack Benny that question. He'd probably place his hand on his chin and roll his eyes upward while turning his head to the side. That's a comic pause of epic proportions.

A skilled comedian can make as much of an impact on an audience with silence as he can with a funny line. Similar to telling a joke, the success can depend on how it's delivered.

"Silence is golden" is not just an old saying. It's also a reminder that "the art of saying nothing" is there to be used to your advantage when performing comedy. Oliver Hardy's silent fuming over Stan Laurel's bumbling antics said more about his stress level than we could ever describe in words. Conversations between Tom and Dick Smothers ending in silent looks toward the audience said more about their feelings during the Vietnam War era than many political commentaries.

A comic pause can be described as an emphasis. Silence at the beginning, middle, or end of a spoken line can add an accent to the meaning. It highlights the part of a comic's bit that is meant to get a laugh:

(Pause) "I never said I drank all the time."
"I never said I drank (pause) all the time."
"I never said I drank all the time." (Pause)

It's very easy to relate comedy to music. How you "play" the dialogue has just as much of an effect on an audience as how a musician "plays" his instrument. There's a reason why music is written with instructions for pauses, timing, volume, accents, and tempo. It allows the composer to bring feeling and meaning into the presentation—which is what you want to do with comedy:

"I couldn't get a decent nap today (pause, then louder), because everyone in the office was *working!*"

The best opportunity to learn delivery techniques is by performing in front of live audiences. A line or joke that didn't work one night might get a huge laugh the next because the comedian altered its delivery. It could be a very slight change, like taking a pause before the punch line and adding an emphasis where it hadn't been before. This might happen for a variety of reasons on that particular night. One might be that the comedian is not afraid to experiment—or another could be out of sheer frustration because he knows it's a good joke, but audiences hadn't been "getting it."

How you get there, whether it's trial and error or planning ahead, is not important. The end result is what counts.

This is another reason why you should always tape your act. Of course it's important to review the jokes that didn't work in an effort to make them better, but also examine the ones that were successful and learn why. It could be that some of the material worked because of a better delivery, and you'll want to use that style for future shows.

There are times you might want to think like a director and plan for pauses. This means you've gone over your act, practiced it, and made an educated guess where a pause would be effective before taking it on stage.

I've seen managers go over new routines with their comedians and make suggestions for pauses and delivery techniques. I've also been known to make people aware of this during my workshops. If a comedian is doing a routine, and a certain line or word really needs emphasis to make it stand out, I'll tell her to consider a pause. But the best way to find out if it's effective or not is by on-stage trial and error.

Listen to the audio tapes of your shows. Pay close attention to your delivery, and if the material is not getting the laughs you think it should, try different ways of saying things. If a pause gives it an added punch, keep it in the act. If you're working with pauses and delivery, audience laughter will be a good indicator about the funniest way to do it.

Lewis Black

On a complicated, "comedy is math" side of this, the pause is basically used to create tension. So it's partly how long the pause is. You essentially create the tension and then it's a matter of just when you think the audience is ready to hear the punch line.

If you want to know about pauses, just watch Jack Benny because he was the master. He was the best. Nobody else had it like him. And you learn. It's really like learning music. It's a rhythm thing in part—and it's a sense of where the audience is at. I had to work on it.

The problem with the pause is that every new comic, you know, panics over silence. And it takes a long time for you to realize that silence is actually your friend.

FAQ 20 **What's the Deal about Using a Callback?**

I've heard comics talking about using callbacks. I understand it as using the same punch line again later in your act. Since I talk about a lot of different things, it doesn't seem like I should be "calling-back" a joke I did earlier if it doesn't relate at all to a following subject or bit. Care to elaborate? —G.F.

Our youngest son and quite a few of his age-group cronies think callbacks are the funniest things in the world. The problem (and reason behind his dad's occasional embarrassment) is that his comedy bits stem from a "digestive system" point of view. An earlier meal at a fast food restaurant can be recalled with a loud belch, sending his friends into giggling laugher and me apologizing to anyone within earshot.

That might be a definition more suited for television's Food Network, but it'll also serve our purposes. A callback is a line or reference to a subject that was used—for laughs—earlier in a comic's act. Hopefully, it's more creative than a belch following a big meal, but if that's what the audience likes . . .

Using callbacks adds continuity to a routine and allows an audience to become more familiar with the performer. A repeated line or reference will give more insight into the comedian's personality and outlook—regardless of the topic. He could be talking early on about apples and later about oranges, but still come to the same result. When this happens, the audience will be reminded of what they laughed about before and are sharing that moment again with the performer.

For example, an earlier bit could have been about his neighbor. The punch line might be: "Then his dog bit me!"

Later, the comic is talking about a different subject. It could be anything, but if there's a slight chance a dog could be involved (real or imagined), he can callback the earlier line. Let's say he's stopped by airport security. After describing his ordeal, instead of ending with a new punch line he can callback the earlier one and say: "Then his dog bit me!"

This tells the audience that maybe the comic has a habit (real or imagined), of being bitten by dogs, which reveals more about the "real" person. It's also a reminder of the earlier material and ties the sections together.

There are also no rules that say callbacks have to relate to different bits. A comic might spot an audience member's shirt and comment that it reminds him of the soup he had for lunch. Later, for no apparent reason, he might notice someone else's shirt and say it reminds him of the soup the other audience member had for lunch. The basic idea is to play off an earlier laugh for another one.

Of course the main reason for using callbacks is to get equal or bigger laughs than the line or reference did the first time around. The audience has already found it to be funny, but now there's the added impact of hearing it again in a different context. It's a shared memory of past laughter and when used correctly will be more effective than this dad's apologies next time he takes his son to a fast food restaurant.

Rocky LaPorte

I've had people come up and go, "Hey, I like how you tie everything in. In this nice little package." Not only do I like callbacks, but I think audiences like them.

I've actually had people come up to me and go, "Hey, what about . . . ?" A lot of times they'll give you bad ones, but every once in awhile they'll come up to you and go, "Hey, what about this?" I've gotten some good callbacks from people in the audience, you know? Like, they'll tell you something after the show. I think people enjoy them—and I enjoy them.

I like when you get the audience into the rhythm. I do all this stuff about my uncles, and at the very last one they think they're all in on it (knowing what's coming next). And then you throw them the curve ball. I like that. It's fun.

Callbacks are lines that get a bigger laugh the second time you use them. But you know what? I don't think callbacks are like a button to push. A lot of people might say, "Ah, it's just like you're pushing buttons." But I think people enjoy them. I've called back stuff from other people's acts and they'll laugh. You know what I mean?

Like an earlier act will be doing something about—whatever. Then you go up there and you mention it and they laugh. It's like, "Oh yeah, I remember that!"

It's like bringing back, "Hey, remember the time me and you did this or that?" You know? And I think people like that stuff.

FAQ 21 When Are Too Many Tag Lines Too Many?

I understand a tag line is an added-on line at the end of a joke. I think they can be funny, but also a little hackish if there are too many at one time. When that happens, I hear more groans than laughs. It's like I don't know when to stop. Are there a certain number of tag lines for one joke that's acceptable, like the "rule of three" that comics talk about? —A.S.

We're lucky there aren't rules about the acceptable number of tag lines that are recognized by society in general and not just for comics. I'm sure parents, teachers, and the IRS would appreciate limiting the number of excuses they hear about why something wasn't done as expected.

There's no such recognition in comedy. A good performance can offer a sense of freedom. If something works, there's no rule to say you can't do it again or improve on it with a tag line if you think it fits. But it's wise to follow a personal rule that's recognizable by the sound of silence or groans from an audience. When that's the reaction, you've probably taken your freedom a little too far and need to pull back a bit for the next show.

"The Rule of Three" you mentioned most often refers to listing items in a comedy bit. Unless each is progressively funnier, it's common to list only three—with the last being the funniest:

"My husband, my kids . . . my boyfriend?!"

When you go beyond three, it might seem the audience is waiting too long for the next laugh. As always in the free comedy world, it all depends on the performer and the material. If they continue to laugh—you can continue to list.

It's the same theory behind tag lines. If it fits your style of comedy, go for the laughs (and in this next example, pretend the laughs are actually there!):

"My husband . . . And my kids!" (laugh) "*And* my boyfriend!" (laugh)
"*And* my boss!" (laugh) "*And* my parole officer!" (laugh)

If for any reason the final "tag" (parole officer) consistently doesn't get a laugh, then the rule of common sense dictates you drop it from the bit and go with two tag lines. If it does, then you have three tags lines that work.

A good tag line can continue a thought or change it completely to surprise the audience. The bottom line is whether or not it gets laughter. But rather than me continuing to tag onto this explanation, I'll refer to the following expert. Tag—you're it!

Wendy Liebman

When I was eleven, I saw Phyllis Diller on a talk show. I think it was Merv Griffin. She said you have to hit the audience with a joke and just when they think they're done laughing, you have to hit them harder. And I remember thinking to myself, at eleven: Yes, Phyllis, I get that. So I guess I always had that style of comedy in me.

I started doing comedy in Boston. I watched as many comedians as I could, and I guess I fashioned my style after Don Gavin, Jonathan Katz, and Bill Braudis—comedians who used tag lines. Since I hated being on stage in silence, I would keep adding jokes to keep the momentum of the laugh going.

Someone recently said I reminded them of Emo Phillips because I'll say something, but the whole meaning will change with the last word:

"I still talk to my ex-boyfriend. We reminisce about the good old day."

"I love to shop . . . lift."

FAQ 22 Does a Funny Voice Make a Funny Character?

I've struggled for awhile doing different characters on stage. The feedback I've gotten from other comics is that they aren't exaggerated enough. It's not enough just to do a different voice, but also to add physical characteristics. Care to comment? —D.M.

You may not realize it, but I'm commenting right now in a character voice. Of course the character is myself, but I have a talent for doing it better than anyone else, so I'll keep it in my writing act.

The most important aspect of doing characters is to become as much of that person, the character, as you can during performances. Yes, this requires some acting ability, but so does a lot of stand-up. Whenever you do an accent or imitate someone you've observed or invented, you are most likely adding that person's voice inflections and mannerisms into your routine. It's not Shakespeare, but as far as we're concerned, it's acting.

Characterizations can bring diversity and detail to your performance. It makes no sense to only go halfway with this, especially when there's a good opportunity to get more laughs from an audience. Imagine you were doing an upscale, overly formal sophisticated-type person that was the complete opposite of who you might be on stage. The bit could be funny with strong material, but the audience reaction would probably be better if you took on a stiff, pompous stance and delivered it with an assumed self-importance that the character might have. This would be a better demonstration of what you are trying to explain while adding personality to the situation. It also can make a laid-back performing style more exciting, or pull back the on-stage energy level to give a real variety to the act.

For example, think of Richard Pryor doing his urban delivery, then becoming the straight-laced Caucasian who is the complete opposite. Jackie Gleason was hysterical as the loud-mouthed Ralph Kramden, but also got big laughs when he became the meek and mild husband whenever Alice grew tired of his antics on *The Honeymooners*. It wouldn't have been as funny if either had only gone halfway with their characterizations.

George Carlin

The answer is individual, depending on the person. There are some characters who don't require a lot of physical support with your body, your hands, or your face. Because the voice that you choose or the intensity that you put into it, the belief, the truth . . .

It's the truth of being the character. And this isn't an acting trick. This is where characters are supposed to come from. They're supposed to come from other parts of you that are very real. Even though they're imagined, they have a very real sense.

One of the things you notice doing characters . . . And I don't like doing them, although I'm really very good at doing characterizations and voices and things. It scares me because when I start, it gets so good that these characters write for themselves. They run the vocabulary. They run the thought process. Anybody who's slipped into a character and just ad-libbed knows that. That suddenly when you talk like an Englishman, you're using things that only Englishmen use in their speech. And references that only come from there. It's a form of alter ego. It's a form of multiple personalities. I mean it's a very primitive form of it, you know. But you have to believe. The character has to be real. If the character is real, then the intensity level will take care of itself. What it needs to be.

If the question is just sort of artificially getting louder or waving your arms more; that probably wouldn't be the answer. The person in question should experiment with the mirror. I was doing things in front of my mirror at home when I was a kid. It always helped me to be an audience and a performer at the same time. It's just a matter of how intense these characters are in you, as to whether they need a lot of support. And some comics who are louder and more extroverted and more out-going and demonstrative, even in their own personas on stage, then their characters have to match that.

If a guy is very low-key . . . Like if a guy had a Steven Wright kind of a sensibility on stage and he did a character, all it would require would be doing and believing in the character to have him stand out. You wouldn't have to suddenly become Robin Williams, you know.

Mike Epps

I do a lot of characters. That's my thing. I do a lot of characters I've seen growing up; a lot of old men in the 'hood. A lot of my cousins. A lot of my uncles, aunties, grandmother, old ladies . . .

I make a story up, right? I'll have three or four characters in the story and I'll act them all out for the audience. It's really like how Richard Pryor used to do it, where he would do three or four characters in one story. There ain't too many people who can do that. I really get into them.

Hey, that's very hard to do. I also do a theatrical one-man show with seven characters. It's the same person, but I show seven different stages of his life. What changes him and what gives him a twist is the shit that he's talking about.

What people don't understand and what helps you get into a character is what you're talking about. If I'm telling you that my mother is saying one thing, and then another person says something else . . . When I do that, then you tell me if that ain't two different people. But it's the same person telling you, but with two different emotions. That's what makes an actor and that's what makes a great comedian. His emotions. To be able to switch emotions.

FAQ 23 How Much Work Is It to Work the Audience?

I just got back from seeing Howie Mandel perform in Las Vegas. All I can say is that I have my work cut out for me. To say the least, it was a great show. I've seen him twice before and he always seems to "connect" exceptionally well with the audience. I know a lot of it is experience and being able to rely on true and tried verbiage, but I understand now how important it is to work off the audience. It gave me a wake-up call on how much work I need to put into my act to *sound completely spontaneous and natural—and still be original and funny, of course. —J.W.*

It's almost impossible to imagine a comedian going from regular open-mike performances to headliner status—unless he buys a club and books himself, which is not unheard of. Even then the bills have to be paid, so if he lacks the drawing power of a Howie Mandel or even the act that sold-out a competitor's club the week before, I doubt he'll be in business too long without scheduling some "big names."

To become a "big name" in the comedy biz you'll most likely have to start at the beginning level, which is as an MC. Since one of the job's requirements is to make the customers feel welcomed, comfortable, and part of a live show, this position offers the chance to gain experience in working off the audience. An MC can talk with members of the crowd, ask questions and improvise a line or bit around their replies to get bigger laughs.

This is why many feature and headline comics have an ability to work off an audience. They started as MCs and had valuable stage time to practice their technique. Jay Leno was an MC at the New York Improv, while Richard Belzer and Bill Maher did the same on a regular basis at New York's Catch A Rising Star. The on-the-job experience helped sharpen their ability to improvise around what an audience member might say, which not only guarantees the act will be different each night, but can also be considered a writing session. An ad-libbed line, either from the comic or someone in the audience, might be so funny it can be used when writing new bit. Working off an audience keeps your mind active, and the thought process funny.

This topic is one that never fails to come up during my comedy workshops. Most beginning comics are concentrating so hard on writing material, they forget the audience is an important part of the show. Sometimes the audience will laugh at all of the jokes, but other times the performer has to work harder for their attention. Keep in mind that stand-up can include a lot of acting, but it's also a very different art form. There is no "fourth wall" (meaning an imaginary barrier between the performer and audience), as there is in acting. A comedian is conversing with a group of people, where an actor is doing a scene or private moment that an audience is witnessing, but not necessarily playing a part in.

Some people are born with a talent for working off an audience. They can talk to anyone about anything and make if funny. They're blessed with a quick wit and are not afraid to use it or base a comedy show around this ability.

Robin Williams, Don Rickles, and Charles Fleischer can walk on stage without preparing a set routine and leave after performing one of the funniest shows many audiences will ever see.

If you don't possess this gift of gab (one way to find out is if you moan, "I shoulda said this!" too many times after your shows), then you'll have to put some work into developing this technique. Start out by taking a few minutes of your act to ask members of the audience questions. The comedy standards have always been:

"Where ya from?" and "Whaddya do for a living?"

Of course we all expect you to be a bit more original than that, at least after you've built up your confidence on stage. You can ask who they're sitting with and why (spouse, date, friend, foe, or designated driver), what they've ordered from the menu (expensive or cheap), do they have any kids, special interests—whatever. Use your imagination, but be interested in what they say, follow your instincts, and hope for the best. You might come out with a few good zingers, or may be an audience member will say something funny. In that case, it's easy to just nod your head in agreement while everyone laughs.

If it makes you feel better to have the odds in your favor, do a little home-work before taking the big plunge into the unknown. Prepare yourself to be spontaneous. Look into the location where you're performing, because chances are the majority of the audience will be from that area and know about local places and events.

Is it a large city or small? What are certain states, cities, and towns known for? Is there anything in particular that may have happened in the past or currently going on that you can comment about? Are there certain places that have reputations you can poke fun at? Does the area have a specific product that is manufactured there or stores where everyone might shop? What about sports teams, museums, or schools? Every place has "something" about it—you just need to know what it is and work it into your ad-libs when the opportunity arrives.

For example, let's choose a few locations and use what we know about them to ad-lib:

New York City "Weren't you the guy on the subway I gave a dollar to last week? If I had known you were going to spend my money here I would've told you a joke and saved a buck."

Los Angeles "You look like you're having about as much fun as I did during rush hour on the 405 Freeway."

Orlando "Are you feeling out of place because no one in here is wearing Mickey Mouse ears?"

Green Bay "Sorry, I didn't realize you were from here without a piece of cheese on your head."

It doesn't matter where someone says they're from or even if you've never heard of the place. This will give you a few more questions to ask:

"Where's that?" or "What's it near?"

Then go into whatever you might know about that area, or just let the audience member talk before commenting on the information given to you. If you really don't know anything about where that person is from or are stuck for words, continue your detective work:

"What do you do there for fun?" or "Should I have heard of it? Why?"

When you have a dialogue going, chances are something will be said to give you an opportunity for a laugh. If not, ask another person what they know about the subject and explore their opinion. It could be contrasting or the same, and you could comment about that fact.

Working off an audience by ad-libbing or improvising takes talent—but so does writing comedy material. Experience counts and (supposedly), the more you do it, the better you'll get at it. But in case of an emergency and nothing said strikes your funny bone, there's no need to dial 911. Another technique is to relax and have some pre-written material as a backup plan:

"I spent a week in (name your city) one night." —W.C. Fields

Depending on what book you might be reading on Fields, the city could have been Philadelphia, Cleveland, or Buffalo. The choice doesn't matter because any city he was talking about at the time could have been used, and the line was still funny.

There's no rule that says a comic's ad-libs can't be pre-written. Making the line appear spontaneous depends on how it's delivered. If you think Don Rickles only called one person a "hockey puck" throughout his entire career, then you need to get out more.

This is another writing exercise you can start right away. Think about the general area where you plan to perform. What's the climate like? ("The heat down here affects you, doesn't it?") In what type of neighborhood is the comedy club located? ("You're a little more sophisticated than everyone else. I see you wore shoes.") What is the approximate age of the person you're talking with? ("When you're out of school and in the real world, you're still expected to answer questions.") The examples could be endless. All you need to do is open your mind to what is around you.

The same could be said about occupations. ("Whaddya do for a living?") Make a list of common jobs and your thoughts about them. Many already have stereotypical reputations, which is obvious if you know any jokes about lawyers or politicians. (Did someone mention "dishonest" as a running theme? Not me . . .), Or you might ask questions to get more specific about what that person's job is. ("Does that ever keep you awake at night—or even when you're working?")

As you continue performing, chances are you'll get answers from the audience that you've never dreamed of. This is where experience counts. You might find yourself without a comeback on different occasions, but if you learn from it and prepare in advance, chances are you'll be ready next time. The whole idea sbehind giving prior thought to ad-libs is to help get the odds in your favor.

Working off the audience and ad-libbing is also a great way to keep their attention. Sometimes an audience will lose focus for any number of reasons, including your material not working at the moment. I've also witnessed small earthquakes, a waiter dropping a tray of drinks, and the dreaded "check spot" (defined in the box in this chapter called, "What They're Really Trying to Say"). Making comments about what is going on in the room at that moment can draw their attention because they don't want to miss the chance of experiencing something spontaneous and funny.

Charles Fleischer

Other than Jonathan Winters, the main inspiration for my comedic reality is Groucho Marx. It was his ability to do ad-lib and say, "Well, I like my cigar too—but I take it out once in awhile."

I was always very much impressed and amused by real-time wit. When you go to see a show and you know it's different than the one before, that presents an aspect that can be considered more interesting or entertaining. I remember one time a couple left the 8 P.M. show and bought tickets for the 10:00 show, because they knew it was going to be different. It's just a little more exciting to me that way.

It's certainly okay to do your act from A to Z, because that's the essence of theater. You're in a play and you do the same play every night. However, it may be done slightly different. You may say the line [English accent], "Guenivere, why have you left the red bag in the shade of the nylon tick?" And the next night you may say, [Southern accent] ". . . the shade of the nylon tick?" So that's the essence of theater, to take something that is rehearsed and regulate it and make it appear as if it is real time.

I consider my act a form of theater. I think that's the thing that separates me from the general group of stand-up performers. I have a theatrical base from which my various streams flow.

You have to maintain your power position on stage, otherwise you lose all credibility. I can only, as you say "go after someone," if they deserve it. If you go after someone vulnerable, the audience will hate you. To create an analogy, if you're watching a movie and someone punches a little old lady in the mouth, you're gonna hate that person. But if in the scene before, you saw that little old lady kill that kid's puppy, then you're gonna cheer. I can't punch someone unless they've killed a puppy. So basically, if someone is a doctor and they don't know a basic medical fact, then that gives me a reason to perhaps question them and be a little more acerbic to them.

I don't think I was always like that, because to have an extensive database requires input. But that's my job. Plus, I am kind of a knowledge junkie. I love information, so it's kind of easy to propel my desire to learn. One thing I take some pride in saying is that I believe I speak to many different levels of the hierarchy. While doing my show, I can make references to perhaps something literary or scientific. And in the same show, we can talk about something that everybody understands. Even though they may not understand one aspect of it, it all blends in and reaches lots of levels. So I could have a joke that has many levels to it and gets laughs from everyone, but a few people would laugh at a few extra points.

I think you should probably strike everything I just said. If you put that down, no one will show up!

I don't base my comedy on physical appearances. It's more on what people do and how they weave into the web of society. What I really try to do from the random

What They're Really Trying To Say

- **Last Call.** In comedy clubs, nightclubs, and bars, last call is the final opportunity customers have to order a drink. After everyone is served, checks are tallied and paid, the show ends, and the club closes for the night.

- **Check Spot.** The check spot comes right after last call. This is the time when the waitstaff presents totaled bills to all the customers at the same time to be paid before the show ends. This prevents any assumed big spenders from blending into the crowd and heading for the exits without paying to play. Inevitably, most of the audience's attention goes immediately to the bill as they divide up what everyone at the table owes, look for adding mistakes, figure out the tip, or go through their pockets looking for cash or credit cards. The unfortunate comedian who is on stage when this happens continues his act despite these distractions until all the checks are accounted for. When the task is complete, he'll get a signal to end the show. If you talk to some comics, they might say check spots have drawn more attention away from the stage than slight earthquakes during shows in Los Angeles.

- **Stretch.** If it takes longer than expected for a bill to be paid, the on-stage comedian will be given a signal to stretch. This is another showbiz term that means to keep the show going until the final customer coughs up the bucks or agrees to a brief career in dishwashing and floor mopping. I've personally given stretch signals to acts that could've used a respirator by the time they got off stage because we were waiting for the last check to come in.

- **In.** What management will say when all the checks are accounted for after last call. It's also what a comedian might say about himself after passing an audition, signing to star in a sitcom, or having an attractive fan at the end of the bar offer to buy a drink.

gathering that forms the audience is to show a web of connectivity that is formed from the knowledge I get from each person. Someone said that they felt what I did was like stand-up literature. It's kind of like the unfolding of a book. You start reading it and the characters in the novel are the people in the audience. So the audience members become characters in this interconnected web that I try to weave, which essentially shows that we are all related in ways that we don't really see until we begin to talk and find out information.

Jonathan Katz

This has to do with working the crowd. I don't think I've ever said it on stage, but I've said it off-stage to other comedians. I don't know what my last words will be, but I'm pretty sure the last words I ever hear will be, "Vinny, he was only goofin' on ya."

FAQ 24   What's the Best Way to Handle Hecklers?

I'm always worried someone is going to shout out something from the audience and just ruin my set. It's happened a couple times before and it really throws off my timing and takes me away from my material. Should I ignore them? Have some pre-written comebacks? —S.K.

This is a true story I'm almost afraid to tell. But since I've matured (physically, if not mentally), and it comes with a moral . . . well, what the heck(ler).

When I was in college, a group of us went to a professional minor-league baseball game. It was in a very small ballpark, and our seats were right behind the visitor's dugout, which made it easy for players on the field to hear whatever we might say. It should also be noted that we were frat boys, and it was ten cent beer night.

As the game and brew continued to flow, we decided the opposing team's first baseman could use our coaching advice. He'd made a few bad plays, so we suggested in loud voices that he might try catching the ball for a change. When he continued to ignore us, we yelled out alternative careers he should consider and our definitive opinions on his talent as a ballplayer. After all, we were only trying to "help" in any way we could. Plus, we thought we were funny.

Toward the end of a losing effort and endless criticism from us, the ballplayer reached his breaking point. He threw down his glove and stormed toward our seats in a rage. His teammates tackled and held him down while he called us names that shouldn't be used outside of a locker room. The umpires threw him out of the game, but if memory serves me correctly, I'm sure we were smart enough to leave the stadium before he had an opportunity to find us later.

The comedy moral? There are a few. . . .

First, many hecklers actually think they're "helping" the show. They have the opinion (sometimes beer induced) that they're funny and should be heard, or the comic might need someone to work off of. I know it sounds perverse, but after years of managing clubs and asking these "helpers" to quiet down, those were frequent excuses for interrupting a show. From the management and performer points of view, they were just drunk or naturally obnoxious people and should know better.

Second, a comedian should not lose his temper on stage and allow someone else to take over his show. That will only result in an ugly situation and prove to club management and audiences the comedian doesn't have enough experience to deal with hecklers.

So, how do you handle it? One way is to ask for help. There is not a club owner anywhere who wants his room turned into a scene from a disaster movie (unless he has insurance, a can of gasoline, and an alibi—but that's a different scenario).

Many clubs have bouncers or at least a staff that should take care of the situation if it's getting out of hand. When a heckler is too loud and disrupting the show, ask management—from the stage—to help. I've seen comedians refuse to perform until the heckler is either quieted or removed from the club. Yes, it's a very uncomfortable situation, but if it's impossible to work under those conditions, you shouldn't. A good audience will usually take the comedian's side because they've paid money and are there for laughs, not confrontation. Sometimes you need help in maintaining crowd control and do what's best for you, the customers, the show, and the person who will decide if you're booked for a return engagement.

Then again, hecklers can be part of the working environment. It may not happen most nights, but sooner or later you can bet someone will decide to "help" your show. Through on-stage experience and a practiced ability to ad-lib, you should eventually be able to handle at least minor disruptions.

If it's still a mental challenge to think on your feet, take a class in improvisational technique. It may not specialize in audience put-downs, but you'll get valuable training and practice working with ideas and situations you haven't prepared for in advance.

Dealing with hecklers depends on your stage persona. Insult comics relish the opportunity to put someone down. They can move into an attack mode by throwing verbal daggers at their victims and often make it a memorable part of the show—as long as their put-downs are funny.

A more laid-back comic might deliver the same knockout punch with just a look or simple comment such as, "Thanks for your opinion, but I can take it from here." The idea is to let that person know his input is not needed or appreciated.

Yes, many comedians have pre-written comeback lines. Some that are classified as "stock lines" (meaning they've been used so much even audiences know they're not original), are:

"Hey, I don't go to your job and yell at you while you're frying burgers."
"Yeah, now I remember what I was like when I had my first drink."
"If I want any crap from you, I'll squeeze your head."

By no means would I ever suggest you use stock lines. These are only examples of three that obviously worked so well for the writers, others copied them too many times. But it does show how a proven comeback can be a valuable asset when needed.

If it makes you feel more comfortable to have an arsenal of comeback lines prepared for different situations, then by all means write them in advance. Just like your material, they can be tried and sharpened on stage when necessary. But if you enjoy flying by the seat of your pants, wing it during these moments and see how they land. If the line works, you might be able to use it again. If it doesn't, avoid another crash and burn, and ad-lib something else next time.

One rule of thumb is to never—*ever*—give a heckler the microphone. A fatal mistake would be to say, "If you think it's so easy, why don't you give it a try?" Immediately, you'll lose control of the audience. The heckler will have more vocal power than the comedian and make himself heard. If he's beer-powered or simply obnoxious, you could have a hard time getting back the microphone, control, and respect from the audience.

Oh yeah, the final moral to this story? I don't heckle or go to ten cent beer nights anymore. Verbal daggers or angry athletes heading in my direction are reasons enough to maintain my self-control and save any obnoxious comments for a television screen that can't fight back.

Bobby Slayton

It depends on the situation. I don't usually stand there and do repartee with them. When you do that, it kind of encourages them to talk more because then they think that they're actually helping the show. They'll hear a laugh and sometimes try to top you or make a come back. So what I usually do is, you know, in certain terms you just tell'em to shut the fuck up.

Now, very often the reason people heckle me is because I say something that upsets them. I don't usually get heckles from guys. Once in awhile—but more from women. They're like cat-calls because they're upset about something I said. So I just gotta stop the show and call them on it and make them look like an idiot. And try to get a laugh at the same time. That generally shuts them up, you know?

Hecklers don't bother me as much as people who are just talking in the audience and carrying on a conversation among themselves. Because then it's not just rude to me, and I don't really care about that, but it's rude to the audience. Because it's very distracting, you know? So I just try to nip it in the bud the best I can. And very often, if they don't shut-up, they realize that I will kill them. I usually go after them. If somebody starts a fight with me and they get the first punch in, you punch them back and knock them out. And even though I knocked him out, I'll still keep kicking him until he's dead.

I guess I was always able to think quick on my feet, but I got better over the years. You know, you can learn how to direct something. It's almost like using misdirection. I think that a comic, if you're good, you can almost direct the heckler into where you want him to go. If they say something, I can either change the subject and start talking to them or just call them on the shit that they're giving me. So you can sort of direct the conversation, if you know what you're doing. It's just something that comes with time. There's no rhyme or reason to why it works. There's no formula for why it works. I don't think it's

something you can learn if you take a comedy class. I just think it's something you learn to do when you do it all the time. It's almost like second nature. It's instinct, you know?

FAQ 25 If I Die on Stage, Will I Ever Live Again?

I died a horrible death on stage last night. Nobody laughed at anything I said, even though a lot of it has worked before on other audiences. I'm confused and dejected over being rejected. Maybe I should become a poet. Was I fooling myself before? How can I prevent this from happening again? —T.J.

I personally don't know any comic who hasn't bombed at one time or another. Usually, it's more often than they'd care to admit, but if they had never suffered on stage we'd lose a lot of great stories about hell gigs, riding an emotional roller coaster, and money spent on therapy.

Each performance, good, bad, or ugly, should be a learning experience. If it's successful, understand why and build on it. When it's a failure, do the same—only different.

If the material has worked on other audiences, you could simply be having an off-night. It could also be the audience, since any group of people can take on its own personality, just like an individual. They might be tired from seeing too many other comics; more interested in the friends they're sitting with; or have a similar taste in humor that doesn't include anything you're talking about. Keep in mind that a roomful of college students is much different than a roomful of college students with their parents.

The answer could be an immediate on-stage adjustment in your delivery style or material. A performer's mental, physical, or vocal energy, whether it's adding more or cutting back, can make a difference. For example, when it seems you're not really interested in what you're saying, chances are the audience won't be either. If your act is loud and confrontational, and the audience appears more uncomfortable than amused, try being more conversational in getting your point across—and vice versa.

Talk to the crowd and learn with whom you're dealing. If you have a variety of topics, do your best to find one that will interest them. If your material can go from "clean" to "not-so-clean" to "anything goes," do some editing in your head and try to give them what will work at that moment.

As I say quite often, the bottom line is to remain true to yourself as a comedian. If the audience wants you to take your material and language to a level you find unacceptable, bite the bullet, and stick to your guns (I can hear Clint Eastwood whistling right now). But never coast or sleep-walk through your act. Stage time is too important to waste. Talk with them and try to find a way to make a bad situation funny. It may not always work, but you'll gain experience as a performer. The positive is that you'll walk away with a determination to write better material and make adjustments to what you already have to cut chances of bombing in the future; plus, you'll gain a tougher skin and knowledge of what type of crowd or clubs to avoid at all costs.

It's the nature of the business that there will undoubtedly be better shows than others, even if your performance and material never varies. Some audiences will "get it" and others won't. Your goal as a successful comedian is to be funny and entertaining night after night—regardless of who is sitting in front of you. When it doesn't work, your job is to figure out why and what you can possibly do to prevent it from happening again.

Yes, the audience is a barometer for how well you're doing, but it's a combination of all your shows and not just one or two. In the beginning, everyone experiences a few bombs going off. It's just that the good ones learn from experience how to keep the fuses from being lit.

George Wallace

I've never bombed a lot. I bombed one time, which was the greatest experience of my life. I wasn't even on the circuit yet. I was about three months into the act, and I went up to a hotel in the mountains in New York and had to be on stage for forty-five minutes. And they put me on stage—and I was even a character then. I was The Reverend George Wallace with the yellow pages as my Bible. And I bombed so bad . . .

I was on stage for forty-five minutes and didn't get one laugh. It hurt so bad. It hurt so bad that I wanted to drive off the bridge coming home. It was horrible! And so that's the great experience I had, because no matter how bad a show can ever get, I can always look back and go, "Well, it wasn't as bad as that!"

Oh, that was a real bomb. But that's why you can learn from everything. I learned a lesson from that. Now I just go up to have a good time. You can't bomb when you're having a good time. When you're laughing and having a good time, it's gonna make those people want to laugh with you.

Part Three OFF STAGE

3 OFF STAGE

FAQ 26 **Can I Stop People from Stealing My Jokes?**

Call me paranoid, but I'm worried about other comics stealing my material. Can you copyright comedy material so that doesn't happen? It's gotten to the point where I'm almost afraid to do my best bits on stage because I worry someone else will start using them in other clubs. I'm still new at doing stand-up and have heard stories about this happening. —J.L.

"Hold on there pardner. There's only room in this comedy town for one joke about airline food—and it's mine. On the count of three, reach for your punch line."

Actually, the legal system has progressed beyond the need for dueling punch lines. A trusted lawyer (why do I feel like every comic reading this has just written a new bit?) can give you the facts about copyrighting. There are options for material that is "fixed" (written down) or only delivered verbally. A one- or two-line joke might be too short, while a sequence of arranged jokes would be eligible for a copyright. There are forms, fees, and other requirements to protect your material, but when you're starting in this business, it's probably better advice to save the extra work and put the effort into being a good comedian. Once you're known among other comics and bookers, the material will be known as yours.

Good comics are known for their best bits. It would be foolish to perform a routine by Eddie Murphy or Adam Sandler when everyone in the audience—especially the club bookers—already know it by heart. Chances are you won't get a return engagement, and "hack" will be added to your reputation.

With lesser-known comics, their jokes are . . . well, lesser known. There's no guarantee that a talent-deficient performer might take the liberty of adding it to their act. But you shouldn't be paranoid about it, thanks to The Honesty Policy that most comics rely on.

Comics have been known to police each other's acts. If you're doing a bit that's unusually similar to someone else's, you can bet a good Samaritan will mention it. Even if it's only to save you from future embarrassment. If it continues and it's obvious you're borrowing more than writing, word-of-mouth will spread, and you might as well consider your day job a career because no one will want to work with you.

For instance, I remember a comic from my days in New York City who was working his way up through the open-mike scene. He was decent, but not ready for major club work, so it caught everyone's attention when he started booking headlining shows out of state. Eventually, a comedy policeman (another comic) saw one of these performances and reported back that he was doing the best material he'd heard from other comics at the open mikes. To make a long story short, I'm pretty sure his current career is telling jokes around an office water cooler, or parking cars.

Of course I'm not naïve and I know this happens, so your best bet is to make your material as individual as possible. If it's more general and observational, trust the comedy police. As you make connections and become known for your act, others will stand up for you. After all, they would want you to do the same for them.

There might be times you write a joke that is completely original to you, but later find it's too similar to someone else's. When you think about it, there are only so many topics in the world, and we all have our own thoughts about them. Sometimes, they're the same thoughts—and we stick to our guns when it comes to ownership.

A general rule says if a comic does a joke on television, it belongs to him. No matter how similar it is to yours, once a viewing audience sees it they'll relate it to the person who told it. You might as well toss the bit out and write something else.

Another story? Glad you asked . . .

A very well-known comic I booked in Los Angeles for *A&E's An Evening At The Improv* opened his set with an ad-libbed line based on the color shirt he was wearing. Unfortunately, it was the same joke a friend of mine had been using in New York City—the other side of the country. There was no way either could have known this, but the damage was done. I called my friend, told him the situation, and he kissed that joke goodbye. Once it's done on television . . .

Bill Engvall

I used to talk about that [joke stealing] with other comics. How do you patent your material? You can't. I've got a patent on "Here's Your Sign," but I had to go through, like, Congress to get it. Jeff Foxworthy has a patent on "You Might Be A Redneck." And it's mainly because of our merchandise. The "Here's Your Sign" merchandise.

What we used to do . . . When we would write a bit, we would date it and put it in an envelope. Then we just kept the envelope. That was our patent. And it was also back then, when I was young, there was just an unwritten code that you didn't steal people's stuff. We used to have . . . We used to call them "Comedy Cops." They would police. They'd say, "Hey, that's Engvall's bit," or "Hey, so-and-so's got a bit like that, you might want to call them." And that's how we took care of things.

I'll tell ya what, in this comedy field, people are pretty righteous. It'd be idiotic for someone to start doing "Here's Your Sign," because it's known that it's mine. But I'm sure there are people out there doing the, "Hey, he's stupid . . ." You know. I mean, I don't have any patent on saying the word "stupid."

FAQ 27 **What Am I Gonna Learn by Taping My Set?**

I'm a musician who's making the move into comedy. I plan to get a tape recorder and video camera to really study and improve my act, but can't afford anything high-tech right now. I understand how important these are since I just finished watching a video of my first time on stage—for the second time. Now that the initial shock has worn off, here's my self-critique:

1. *I really need to start going to the gym!*

2. *My timing was off on a lot of lines that I think would've gotten a laugh if I had paused more and accented a few words differently.*

3. *I could make eye contact a little better with the audience; I noticed that I kept looking at the ground, and I think I was more effective when I engaged the audience.*

4. *My material was basically a story, which may not be the best option for a five-minute set. I think this technique will work well for me when I'm doing more time on stage, which is what I really want to do. But for a short set, a more fast-paced, scatological approach with a lot of punch lines might work better. —D.L.*

Let's not get strung too tightly, because it was only your first time on stage doing comedy. Even if you've had a lot of experience with music, going for foot-pounding laughs is a whole different tune (am I jamming with the word-play, or what?!). First of all, don't—and I'll repeat myself—*do not* spend mucho bucks on sophisticated equipment to record your act on a nightly basis. This statement makes a lot of sense, while also demonstrating the extent of my bilingual abilities after two years of high-school Spanish.

Whether it's an open mike or the headlining spot at a major club, the main reason for recording your set is to review what you did during that perform-ance. The idea is to be aware of what material worked and what didn't, your delivery, wording, pauses, and all other aspects of your technique. This is espe-cially valuable when you're working out new material or if you ad-lib a great line or bit. This way, you won't lose it.

I suggest you buy an inexpensive, pocket tape recorder that won't set you back more than two tanks full of gas for your car. (Okay, maybe that's a bad example in this day and age because some of us have paid less in rent at one time or another.) To keep it simple, figure out what it would cost to take all your fans at a really bad open-mike club out to a fast-food restaurant, then set your goal to pay less for a tape recorder. Remember, you're not looking for high-tech quality—it's just for your own learning process.

Basically, you want to hear your material and how the audience reacts. Hopefully it will be with laughter, but silence or groans have been known to teach a few lessons to upcoming comics.

The theory behind staying with an inexpensive tape recorder is based on the fact that you'll probably go through a number of them. The idea is to place it on a table, chair, or speaker near the stage to get a decent sound. Some acts will take it on stage and place it on a stool, which can be good for damage control. Occa-sionally it might get knocked off the table, you'll drop it, or someone with sticky fingers will decide to take it for their own use while you're captivating everyone else in the audience with brilliant comedy material. Whatever the case may be, you don't want to take those chances with anything expensive.

A video camera made for home use can also work as a learning tool, but rarely will the quality be good enough for a promotional tape. Filming a stage lit with spot lights from the back of a dark club will result in an unclear picture, while the small speaker will probably pick up room conversation better than what you say on stage.

When the day comes where you want to record your act to either send out as a promotional tool or to sell as a "live album" after performances, invest the money and hire a professional to do it. Otherwise, your main goal is to make a "work tape" for your own use. And believe me, just about any brand will do, as long as it has a record and playback button that works well enough to hear what you're saying, see what you're doing, and how the audience reacts.

Secondly (if you remember from an earlier paragraph, there was a "first"— this is the "second"), everything you listed can make good sense when critiquing a video. Any changes you make should be personal choices, but always with an eye and ear toward audience reaction. For some general thoughts on a personal level . . .

1. Jackie Gleason didn't worry about going to a gym.

2. Your act should come together gradually with more stage time. Some comedians may improve at a faster pace, while others take years to develop on-stage talents. I'm sure you don't want to waste time, but it's not a bad idea to have some patience. If you can make one small improvement every time you perform, it will eventually add up to a lot of progress.

3. Good timing comes from on-stage experience in front of an audience. All the "greats" have great timing, from Groucho Marx and Bob Hope to Chris Rock and Jerry Seinfeld. They all had on-the-job training and plenty of it. You've only taken the first step of a long journey, but where you're at now will only be a memory as the performances add up.

4. Doing a story for a five minute set? Why not? Bill Cosby and Rondell Sheridan can do it, so with talent, good material, and experience, there's no reason why you can't too. Like everything else in this business, it depends on how much effort you're willing to put into your routine to make it successful.

Whenever I'm ending an interview with a comedian for my newspaper columns, I ask for a joke that can be used to lead into the article. More often than not, this is the toughest question to answer. Not only does it put him on the spot to be immediately funny, but a comic who focuses on stories simply won't have any one-liners or short jokes that don't need more of an explanation than space will allow. Some are not able to do it. Period. Many talk about experiences, observations, and thoughts in a story form that is very funny, but the material won't have a "wham bam joke" to be as entertaining out of context.

Fill your stories with funny lines, details, thoughts, characters, and whatever will help to make it a more funny routine. There's a method to this madness, which you'll discover as you record and study your performances while continuing to grow on stage.

Dave Attell

On taping your show, the way I put it is this way, okay? You bomb in front of the audience—and then you get to hear yourself bomb in front of the audience. So for as much misery as you doled out, you have to take it the next day, hungover somewhere, sitting and drinking coffee.

I guess what they would say is it's kind of like with the Gulf War. You get to see the camera in the bomb, you know? But you're the bomb and you get to see it, like, land and if it went in right or didn't go in right. So that's why I tape. You get to see what went wrong. You get to hear what went wrong.

FAQ 28 Should I Enter Comedy Contests?

Last night I won first place in a comedy contest. The $250 prize money was as much as I had made in the past year of doing stand-up. I didn't have a lot of people there to support me (most of the audience was there for other performers), which makes me feel good about winning. There were also a second and third place winner, but I honestly think they picked the three of us because we stuck to the rules. One guy who was really funny and unique went over the five minute maximum and was disqualified. Another, who could've placed, swore—and that was against the rules. I don't get these guys, because the manager gave us all a paper with the rules and went over them with us. Sheesh!! All in all, I'm happy with it—and being recognized is an added bonus! —T.L.

First of all, I don't go to the horse races very often because . . . well, I'm married and my wife had that stipulation put in our wedding vows. But I do have a faint recollection that hitting "win, place, or show" can be a big deal. Winning $250 "ain't no chump change" (to use an expression from my bachelor days), and it's a prize you should be proud of. The amount won't fill your retirement fund, but it's enough to let you hang around the winner's circle for a while and an excuse to let people know you're there.

By the way, that excuse is called promotion. We'll get to that in a moment, but right now I'm on a roll. . . .

Comedy contests, like horse races, are a lot more fun to win than to lose. Winning can build your confidence and add an impressive stat to your track record. But it's only one race in a career that can better be described as a marathon.

Now that I've made all my innuendoes and inside jokes, I'll stop jockeying around with the horse sense and start the home stretch for the finish line. After all, it's a career in comedy that we're training for.

Without adding the unnecessary pressure of "winning" to the situation, you should look at comedy contests as another opportunity to gain valuable stage time. This is especially true if it's difficult to find open-mike rooms in your area, or when the more prestigious comedy clubs are run on tight, pre-booked schedules with no time to offer regular audition nights. It's possible some of these clubs will run comedy contests. Your job is to call and find out.

When you learn a club is having a contest, don't hesitate to follow the guidelines and sign up as a contestant. Often there are only a certain number of spots available, and you don't want to miss an opportunity by taking time to think it over. Performers who are more aggressive in finding stage time could take it and when the space is filled, your "waiting and debating" could be another unnecessary delay in climbing the ladder to success.

Okay, I can almost hear sarcastic one-liners coming at me from experienced comics wanting to debate my "not wait" advice. I know they have legitimate reasons, but all I ask is that you give me a chance to finish the race.

As always, you must be honest with yourself in terms of how your act is being received by audiences. This is especially true before competing in a contest at a club where you someday hope to be a regular performer. If you've never done your act on stage in front of an audience, it's important to first get that experience somewhere else. Start with an open mike or a workshop as the learning process. If you're anywhere near civilization, it shouldn't be too difficult to find a club that has live entertainment. Be aggressive and ask to perform a short set—for free—while the performer is on a break. The worst thing they can do is say no, which should only make you more determined to find another place more worthwhile to spend your time, cover charge, drink minimum, and humorous personality.

If it's a local nightclub that doesn't specialize in booking big-name comedy acts and might be "giving comedy a try," as club owners often say, it shouldn't have any effect on your long-term career. Whether you win, place, show, or bomb, consider it a learning experience, which is always an important step in the right direction.

If you've signed-up for a contest and later discover the club has a lousy reputation or other reasons why you definitely would not want to perform there, then cancel. You've at least given yourself the opportunity to debate what you should do—without losing out on the spot while thinking it over. But make your cancellation sound legitimate and not that you heard it's a lousy club. They might someday change that reputation around and remember your criticism as their first impression.

When you enter a contest at a more legitimate comedy club, your first set might make an impression that could stay with you. This is when it's important to be honest with yourself. Go to a couple shows first and see if you have the type of material that will work for the club's audiences. If you're doing an X-rated act and it's a club that attracts families, the booker might not appreciate what you do and remember to never have you back. If you can't go to the club in person, call and ask what guidelines they have for the contests. Very often they'll have rules that range from no profanity to "anything goes." Just be aware of what they expect from the comedians who work there.

If you've done your homework and honestly feel you can compete with the other comics, by all means sign-up and take part in the contest. It's open stage time and you should be aggressive enough to take advantage of it.

Once you're in a contest, how you use the situation depends on what you want from it. If you're still uncertain about portions of your act and are there for the stage time only, it's a chance to work out the problems based on audience reaction—which is what an open-mike room is for. When you're looking to add a winning credit to your résumé, treat it like any important showcase and do your best set. But don't let winning or losing change your aggressive attitude toward performing. The judging at many of these contests can always be questioned depending on how many friends another act has in the audience, or the owner's sense of humor. If you feel you've done your best and earned laughs in the process, you're a winner regardless of who earns the title of "Best Comic on a Tuesday Night in a Club with Four Audience Members All Related to the Person Who Won."

Mark Curry

It's about working the house. It's a good judge of character, but it doesn't make or break you. But it is good to be able to target your material toward the audience for a certain amount of time.

You gotta be very pliable when you write. You know, get all the money! I can play any audience. Any audience well. I can go from kids to white to black, it don't make no difference. Corporate and back again, and can do well. That's the way to do it.

FAQ 29 **Does Anyone Still Believe Comedy's a Man's World?**

Always a bridesmaid and never a bride. For the third year in a row, I was the runner-up in a "Funniest Person" contest. As usual, the guys outnumbered us and think they dominate, but I'm not bitter because those men will get a surprise when I pass them by and wave. We ladies are taking it to them from now on. Taking no hostages! —S.B.

As James Brown once sang, "It's a man's, man's, man's, man's world." Of course he wasn't referring to the male/female ratio in comedy, but that thought hit a power chord in my mind while reading your message.

First of all, it's great you always do so well in these contests—despite your claim of being left standing at the altar while some guy grabs the brass ring. These achievements prove you're a consistent performer and not a one-hit wonder. Winning contests is nice for the résumé, but what do they really mean in the long run? Unless you're winning titles at major festivals or national competitions, I honestly think bookers pay little attention to these credits. There are so many contests with so many winners that it's easy to get lost in the brass ring of champions. The important goal is to get laughs from both audiences and talent bookers. That's what will get you noticed—and hired.

Secondly, stand-up comedy has often been described as a "man's world." Does that mean there are no funny women comedians? I'm sure you already know the answer to that question, so I'll refrain from filling pages listing the funniest females of both the past and present. Some may tell you the male dominance has worked for their benefit, or made it more difficult. But on the flip side of the same song, there are guys who will tell you the same thing: too many men, so funny women are always in demand. The deal is to be funny, which should work in your favor.

Brett Butler

OK, look. If you're funny, it'll happen. I grew up with a funny mom, four funny sisters, and a bunch of funny aunts. It never occurred to me that I was genetically or comedically deficient due to being born female. Comedy competitions are a drag. Stand-up comedy is art—or it's supposed to be. Contests belittle the form and the point of it. However, it's a way of being noticed, so if you're a woman who has a routine, go do it, stand where you live, deliver the best you can and don't you dare walk off feeling screwed if a guy wins. The only thing I can do to change the status quo is be funny and not to quit doing it. Hey, at least we're not women golfers trying to kick ass on some grass out in the hot sun where a lot of men want us to lose. God. There are harder things to prove in life. Have fun, keep writing, and next thing you know, who wins what won't matter. All you'll hear is laughing.

FAQ 30 **How Do You Get a Manager and an Agent?**

I'm relatively new in the comedy business, but I'd like someone to help me get bookings. I should be working in clubs every weekend—and I also want to get on television (because I'm funny!). I need an agent or a manager. What's the difference and how can I get one? —S.T.

Wait a minute! If you're new in the comedy business—or even if you've been around for awhile—why do you think you "need" an agent or manager? Okay, I know the answer—because you want more and better gigs. I would also guess more money. But are you at the point in your career right now where you can afford to *pay* someone else a big chunk of your earnings to do all that? Here are the potential business partners you're thinking about adding to your payroll:

- **A Manager.** A good manager will "groom" you and your act into a position to attract a good agent. He's a co-conspirator, cohort, and codependent when times are good and bad. He can make suggestions about your material, delivery, appearance, and promotion. In some places he can even book shows for you, while in others it's against the law (he'd have to be a licensed agent). But to do this, a manager is paid a percentage of your earnings. How much? Normally 15 percent of everything you do in the entertainment business is a starting point, but sometimes their efforts and good intentions demand more.

- **An Agent.** An agent gets you jobs. Among the ways this can happen are through reputation (how powerful and respected they are in the industry), promotional mailings, showcase auditions, or even lunch with personal or professional contacts. However this is accomplished, an agent dealing with the person hiring for the job you are "right" for does it. An agent can work through a manager or directly with the performer. His fee? A standard figure has always been 10 percent, though two to three times higher have been mentioned when there's big money on the table to be earned.

- **Total Representation.** You figure it out. The bottom line for having both an agent and manager? If my calculator is accurate, we're talking a minimum of 25 percent of *everything* you make as a comedian.

The first thing you need to do is take an honest look at yourself as a comedian and where you are in your career before concerning yourself over having a manager or agent. Are you headlining or at least featuring and getting as many bookings as you possibly can on your own? Are your days consumed by traveling, writing, and performing so there's no time left for you to do both these off-stage jobs yourself? Are you seriously matching up to—or doing better than—the comedians seen on television or headlining the best clubs? If that's the case, then there are two options:

1. Put together a professional looking promo package. (How? It's in this book!) Research managers and agents to find where they are located and what types of entertainers they represent. (Hint: find those who work with comics!) This can be done through the Internet or entertainment industry books that specifically list this information. The best way is through referrals. If you know comics who are happy with their representation (and more importantly—working), ask for a referral or the best way to make contact. Send out promo packages and "stay in touch" (to be described in a moment).

2. Be *so good* that an agent or manager will find *you*. After all, this is a business, and they also have a job to do. If they can put you into a more profitable position, it benefits both parties. Search for clubs in larger cities where agencies and management companies are located. Showcase whenever possible, because you never know who might be sitting in the audience looking for opportunities.

If you don't happen to fit into the above category yet (no life outside of traveling, writing, and performing), then cut the payroll by acting as your own agent and manager. Everyone does this in the beginning, starting with the mental coaxing you needed to step on stage at your first open mike. In fact, that already makes you a "beginner agent."

The job? Okay, but keep in mind that you should already be working as a comic at clubs or events somewhere near your location. We've already talked about open mikes and showcasing, so hopefully this has led you to at least paid spots as an MC, and your performance is ready for other audiences. . . .

1. Never stop trying to become a better comedian. Your goal is to be the best, which means writing and performing. Put together your promotional material, including a video that is a strong representation of your act. This is your job as a manager.

2. Send these packages to bookers and "stay in touch." If this leads to jobs in other areas, do open mikes or schedule showcases at clubs along your travel route. Get yourself or promo material to whoever can get you work. When you get a booking, you're acting as an agent.

During the early stages of your career, there will not be much need for representation skilled at negotiating you a better deal. Most clubs have it in stone what they'll pay for an MC or feature and have no trouble finding someone who will accept it. Your goal is to be "that" act—and be *so good* you become a "returning act." Eventually, your goal is to be the headliner.

If you move into the college or corporate markets (again, either through research and self-promotion or personal contacts), you'll learn firsthand what is acceptable to charge for your performance. For instance, if you ask for $200 and are hired to perform in front of a thousand people in formal dress, and it's obvious they spent more money on table decorations than entertainment, you've priced yourself too low. If you ask for $500 and hear the other person sweating through the phone line, then you have to make a decision. Ask what their budget is and decide if that's an amount you'd be willing to accept.

These are only examples of what you might expect, but these experiences will be invaluable in the long run. There's no reason why you can't book your own shows and save commission fees until business is so good you "need" representation to take you to a higher level. Along the way, you'll become what you set out to be—a professional comedian. You'll also learn what to expect from your future agent and manager. The main idea is to do the hands-on work yourself, until you're in a position where an agent or manager "needs" you.

Bruce Smith (Founder and partner, Omnipop, Inc. Talent Agency)

If you are at the MC, middle, or beginner headliner level, my advice is to have a little backbone and book yourself. Why not develop some business skills and keep that commission in your pocket for a while? An agent or manager can only truly help when your act is ready.

Just organize your picture, bio, and any press materials. Make sure you've got a solid tape of a club-length set, and put the pressure on your comic buddies for referrals. Once you've honed a clear voice and stage persona, you may find yourself stuck at the low-level headliner stage, making $1,000 per week with travel allowance or $1,200 with no travel allowance. That might be a good time to re-evaluate your situation. There are agents who specialize in college or corporate bookings. These agents might be located anywhere in the continental United States—as can you—to take advantage of their services.

If you really want a career in television or film, you'll eventually have to consider moving to New York or Los Angeles. These are extremely competitive markets and you shouldn't even consider this possibility unless you are working at the very top of your game. Without representation, you'll get lost in a sea of unemployed comics and actors who can't get arrested. My advice is to send tapes to a select group of comedy agents and managers before you move. You may seem more like a "discovery" before you relocate and in show business, everyone loves a "discovery." It may be a bit tough getting people to take calls and open packages, but if you are truly talented, someone will recognize it.

Failing to arrive in New York or Los Angeles represented, you must be immediately proactive. Make it your business to find out where every last comedy venue is located and who books it. Get out. Survey the scene. Different rooms have different personalities. Some offer just stage time, while others regularly provide industry exposure. Figure out

Staying In Touch

- **Postcards.** Similar to head shots, only postcard size. Use these to stay in contact with bookers, agents, and managers. It's not as intrusive as a phone call, while having your face, name, and contact information land on their desks every few weeks or once a month. A message on the back can announce career updates or a simple, "Hi–hope you're keeping me in mind for any work."

- **Follow-Up Phone Calls.** After mailing your promotional package, wait about two weeks. If you haven't received a response, make an introductory phone call and ask if they've watched your video. Chances are very good you'll be greeted with a 'No, not yet.' Ask when it might be a better time to call back. Many bookers have specific days and hours they take calls or can estimate when they may have a chance to review your material. Write down the date and time. After hanging up, send a postcard stating your intention to call back–and do it at that specific time. This process may continue for awhile, but you need to be persistent–without being a pain in the you-know-what. Eventually, you'll get an answer.

- **Avails.** A comedian's upcoming schedule. Includes dates you're available for work (hence the name "avails"), and ones you already have booked and are not available. These are normally on one page and could be in a calendar form or a list. Avails are emailed, faxed, or mailed once a month to bookers you've already worked for. If your promotional package or showcase is accepted–meaning they are considering you for work–ask how often they'd like your avails and don't forget to send them in.

where you fit in. Network with other comics and make friends with the bookers. If you want acting roles, join a good acting class. Go to sitcom tapings. Get the system wired. If you are getting stage time and you are unique, the word will spread and you'll attract agents and managers.

As for the age-old dilemma of agent versus manager, ignore it. The answer is to find someone who believes in you, will fight for you, and has the contacts to get the job done. I know great agents and managers, as well as some truly terrible ones. Some are Hollywood clichés and some are bright, funny, soulful people. By strict definition, agents are licensed to negotiate and secure work for you, while managers are unlicensed and relegated to career-planning and organizing. In practice, these definitions rarely hold. Although in some states (New York and California) a manager can get into trouble for booking shows, in most places people just look the other way. There are a lot of agent-like managers and managerial agents. Find the one who works for you. Do not concern yourself with an entourage. You really do not need an agent and a manager unless your career takes off, necessitating a team to cover the complexities.

As for myself and Omnipop, I am only interested in the very best comics. Period. While this seems to state the obvious, I can't stress enough that our culture is riddled with bad taste. You can see it in movies, television, fashion, music, politics, and yes, stand-up comedy. Most comics are regrettably generic, the comedy equivalent of a bad sitcom. I define a great comic as having a unique voice and thought process. In order to crossover, they must have a castable look and acting training. I want people who know who they are, have paid their dues, and are mentally prepared for a challenging career game. Their individual style is of little consequence. The comic could be silly or cerebral, but they better be silly like Steve Martin or cerebral like Albert Brooks. They could be low-key or outspoken, but they better be low-key like Steven Wright or outspoken like Chris Rock. There's no room for more mediocrity. This business is too tough. Heat goes away, but talent doesn't. I always try to invest in the talent.

FAQ 31 When Should I Start Promoting Myself?

Last week I was in Boston for the Boston Comedy Festival. It was a thirteen-hour drive, but it was a good chance for networking. I was talking with another act who said she's too impatient about getting her comedy career going. I said that my problem is that I'm too patient. After finishing second at another comedy club's contest and being accepted in Boston, I should be contacting clubs and bookers all over the area instead of waiting until I actually win a contest. Do you agree? —J.G.

First of all, if I drive thirteen hours for *anything*, I'm going to make sure *somebody* knows about it. That's not exactly a Sunday afternoon drive for me (which is why every seasoned road comic is calling me a wimp right now), so I'd like a little recognition for the achievement. If my kids happened to be in the backseat, I'd expect an award.

How different people react to my successful lengthy trip depends on how they view such an effort. If I told a student driver about my journey, he may look at me as "The Man." If I walked into a truck stop and made my announcement, I'd probably get more laughs than doing a clean act at a biker bar open mike.

Being accepted to perform at a respected comedy festival and finishing second in a club's contest are worthy additions to the résumé. Each step in your career is a great opportunity for promotion and it's important to take advantage of it, which is an important subject we're driving up to next.

But before we head down that road, the question of patience should be answered by common sense. You have to be honest with yourself to know when you're ready for the next level of your career and not push yourself too fast into a position where you don't have the experience or material to back it up. In other words, if you're relatively new to comedy and just breaking into the MC role, it's wise not to promote yourself to the top clubs as a headliner until you're ready.

What you don't want to do is sit back and wait for any word-of-mouth to find its way to the bookers. James Bond has a reputation that precedes him, but when finding work in the entertainment business you need to promote yourself. If you have the credits, chances are better that the bookers will find out about it if *you* tell them.

Jackie "The Joke Man" Martling

I knew that any moron could take a tape, send it away, and have it made into records. So, six months after I started in stand-up, I had a comedy record called, "What Did You Expect?"

After I put out this album, I sent it to everyone I met. I then put out two more albums, "Goin' Ape" and "Normal People Are People You Don't Know That Well," and sent them to everyone. I had no money. I would work a gig for fifty bucks and then use that for postage.

I was working in Washington when a club owner said to me, "This guy just got fired and he's going to NBC in New York. You should hook up with him 'cause he's like you. He's crazy." He told me his name was Howard Stern, so blindly, I sent a package to NBC. A couple of months later he called and said, "We're doing a talent contest over the telephone today, you wanna be a judge? We really love your album and think you're hysterical." So I said, "Sure."

FAQ 32 **What Goes in a Promo Package?**

I did an open mike and someone from the audience said he could help me get paid bookings! He asked me to send a promo package. What should I include? —T.D.

First of all, a promotional package is your job application. The idea is to look professional—which means you present a professional-looking application. With that said, here's what your competition is presenting . . .

- **Head Shot.** An 8″ × 10″ smiling (or frowning, if that's your style) photo of what you look like. They could be called "face shots," since that's usually the main focus. Comics also use half- or full-body poses, a live on-stage picture, or even props if it helps convey their personality or act. Black and white is most common and economical. For examples, find a newspaper advertisement for a comedy club containing a photo of their headliner— and that's a head shot.

- **Résumé.** A listing of performance credits. Includes comedy clubs, corporate and college shows, television, films, awards, training, and any special talents (music, impressions, etc.), that might be included in your act. Beginning comics can list open mikes to show they have experience, then gradually replace with better credits.

- **Bio.** A brief story about yourself. You could include your personal history, comedy influences, why and how you got into the business, a brief description of your performance style, and career highlights. This is a good opportunity to be as creative in your promotional material as you are on stage. In other words, a bio can be entertaining. One hundred and fifty words is acceptable when just starting out, and it's a good idea to keep it to one page until you're almost a household name. Stars and major head-liners can have numerous pages.

- **Video.** A videotape of your act and the next best thing to a live audition. Five to ten minutes in length is acceptable and usually preferred. If the booker is interested, he can ask for a longer tape, schedule a showcase, or (hopefully) hire you. Good picture, sound quality, and a positive (laughing) audience response are important. This item carries the most weight in any promo package and the goal is to make a positive, memorable, and professional first impression.

- **Cover Letter.** Simple. Write a personal introduction letter requesting the talent booker to review the enclosed material. It's also a good idea to include something that says you've heard the venue or booker is the best in the business, and the only goal you have in your entire life is to work there. (At least something close to that!) Ask them to consider you for work or an audition based on your promotional package and that you'll be in touch, which is a business technique we talked about earlier.

- **Contact Info.** Be sure to have your name and phone number on every item in your package. If you use an e-mail address and/or Web site, also include those. Make it as easy as possible for the booker to contact you. The reason you should have this information on each piece of promotional material is in case the pieces get separated. (For instance, videos in one pile—head shots in another, etc.)

- **Going Postal.** Put all the above items in a two-pocket folder (for that professional look) and into a padded envelope. Address, mail, and start work on another promotional package aimed for a different club or booker. Remember, the more people you contact, the more opportunities you'll have.

Your promo package—without a videotape—can also double as a press kit. What I mean is that you might as well get some ink from the media or air time from broadcasters when performing in different areas to make your promo package even more impressive.

Sound too far advanced for where your career is at the moment? It really isn't. If you're doing a paid show somewhere, there's no reason not to consider it newsworthy. I've written newspaper entertainment columns since the last millennium and found you can only interview a returning headliner so many times before each article about them sounds the same. Eventually, reporters and radio hosts might look at the feature or opening acts for a different story idea.

Benefits, contests, and festivals also draw attention. If a reporter is covering the event and interested in singling out a performer, the comic who in advance has a professional-looking press kit (promo package) on his desk could make his work a lot easier.

Do a little research on the Internet or in a library to find newspapers and radio stations in the area where you'll be performing. Send a press kit, follow up with a phone call, and hopefully your collection of press clippings and résumé credits will grow.

Debbie Keller (Owner, Personal Publicity)

You need to personalize your press kits. With mine, the different folders go with the different clients I have. We use their pictures on the front of the press kits. So if they're laying in a pile of other people's press kits, you're going to see their face without having to file through everything. I think it's important to personalize them.

Color slides and color art is always the best way to go for newspapers. Because that really dictates placement a lot of the time. They will take color art over black and white and put that person in a better placement in the paper.

I would also say that their résumé—or as I call it, a tip sheet—is important for radio interviews. It just has everything itemized. The shows they've been on and what they've done is in a list form. It makes it easier for someone doing an interview because they can just go down and ask how a particular show went.

Any recent reviews and articles that have anything to do with the show are help-ful and should be included in a press kit. Reporters find it helpful to look and see what kinds of takes and spins other reporters have taken. It helps them be more creative and maybe go a different way.

FAQ 33 How Do I Get a Good Promo Tape?

I'm looking to get a good promotional videotape that will get me work. What is the best way to tape a show? The cost of hiring a "real" professional is prohibitive, but I know you've said home movie cameras aren't always a good way to go. —S.V.

Common home movie or video cameras are great when used for keeping a visual record of what goes on in your everyday life. This includes family fun, holiday celebrations, or vacations. Also if you happen to be married to Pamela Anderson, which also can be classified as family fun. But when you're looking to promote yourself as a professional entertainer, the resulting picture and sound from a home video camera will probably not be up to the quality of your competition.

It can be very difficult to get a good promotional video. It never hurts to take a home camera with you to performances and ask the club's manager if he will let you tape your set. This is an excellent way to study your act, and it doesn't have to be great quality for that purpose.

When it comes to sending out promotional videos, you should understand that the better the quality, the more professional (and better) you look. Remem-ber, they may call it amateur night, but no one is looking to hire an amateur.

As you already stated, hiring a professional to videotape your performance can be costly. When shopping around, it's important they have a camera that will provide a sharp picture and a microphone not only to record your voice clearly, but also the audience reaction.

I don't always enjoy talking about certain experiences, but sometimes a lesson learned is one to be shared. . . .

A number of years ago, the producer of a major comedy festival called and asked me to recommend comedians from my area. Since he trusted my judgment (not the wisest decision he ever made based on the following confession), he asked if I would put together a showcase, have it video-taped, and send him the results. He also gave me a generous monetary budget for the project, which happened to be close to the price of a new home video camera.

The fact that I had never videotaped anything in a nightclub before was no obstacle in hiring myself as the professional cameraman. For some reason, all the large cameras, lights, production equipment, and makeup people I'd seen at many television tapings didn't register in my mind as being necessary. But I was about to get a lesson in Film Class 101.

The showcase was at a popular comedy club in front of a very responsive audience. At least a dozen acts performed five-minute sets hoping for a big break at the comedy festival, while I taped the show with my video camera from the back of the room on a borrowed tripod. Everything went without a hitch, until I returned home and popped the tape into our VCR.

The first act looked great walking onto the stage from the darkness of the room, but when he stepped in front of the spotlight, his face disappeared. This would've been acceptable if he was auditioning for the role of a ghost, but a complete meltdown for a comedy showcase. Squinting at the screen, I could sometimes detect his mouth opening and closing, but otherwise his head was a shiny blur on top of his body.

Stunned, I fast-forwarded the tape to the next act and discovered the same results. Hoping I could at least hear what he was saying, I instead listened to a waiter taking drink orders and conversations at the table directly in front of my camera.

In the School of Hard Knocks, this turned out to be a valuable lesson. Filming something brightly lit from . . . oh, let's say from the back of a dark comedy club, will cause the lens to go haywire (for lack of a technical term).

The result is not unlike standing in your backyard and filming the sun. Add trivial conversation, clink a few glasses together, and you'll have the same video I had planned to send to a major comedy festival.

In a final plea for leniency from the comedy court, I called the comedians back for a second showcase and hired a professional to tape the show. I also accepted my sentence to share this experience with the world—or at least with comedians who ask me about taping with a home camera.

The important goal is to have a video with the best quality you can possibly get. It's true that performances filmed on a home video camera from the back of a club have gotten comics work in the past. But this method has also caused bookers to hit the fast forward or eject buttons more frequently if the tapes are almost unbearable to watch when compared to more professional ones sent by your competitors.

Of course the best promotional tape to use would be from a television appearance taped in front of a live audience. But if you haven't made your small screen debut yet, here are a couple economical suggestions:

Contact a college or high school close to where you're performing and ask if they have a film or television course that might want a special project. If they can schedule a performance at their school, volunteer to do a show for free. The students can tape your set, get an A in creativity—and you get a copy of the tape.

Or, get together a group of comics who each want a new promotional tape and find a venue that will allow everyone to do a short set. Hire someone to professionally film it and split the cost, which is essentially what happens at my workshop shows. For instance, if the fee is $200—get ten comics and that's only $20 each. It takes some organizing, but when I worked in New York and Los Angeles, comedians were doing this quite often (that's how I "invented" the idea!).

Schedule a particular night to videotape and keep the audience laughing. A positive response is important, which is why some comics will pack the club with friends and family for a more vocal audience reaction. Yes, I know that sounds dishonest, but I feel you and I have a special bond between us, and I can tell you that. Besides, if you're funny, bookers will never need to know the loudest laughers were "plants."

Getting a good promotional video may seem like a lot of work, but it's worth the effort. It's the next best thing to being there in person.

Comedy Knowledge

- **Comedy Savvy.** Knowledge of comedy. In audience terms, it could mean knowing something about the comedian they've come to see, or expecting a certain type of show based on the reputation of a club. For comedians it's understanding the business, knowing what to deliver based on the venue they're playing, or being able to adjust their material depending on the audience.

- **A Plant.** When you want your surroundings to look good, you might go out and buy a fake tree or a plastic bouquet of flowers for the living room. This is not exactly the type of "plant" I'm talking about—but it's close. When you fill an audience with friends and family to get a good response, you've definitely improved the surroundings for yourself. This can also be an audience member that (unknown to the rest of the crowd) a comic brings to the show so they can work off each other during pre-written bits.

Jann Karam

Trying to get a good tape—what a hassle! But you gotta do it.

My advice is to buy a camera, or better yet, become friends with one of those tech geeks who will dutifully follow you around to lots of your gigs and tape your sets. He would probably even love to help you edit! Plus, it's great to have a pal and not have to rely on the club for technical assistance. You could also learn to shoot and edit yourself, which only helps to prepare you for what you really want to do—direct.

Sometimes a videographer will show up at the clubs and tape a bunch of comedians for a fee. If you have the money, take advantage of the opportunity. Tape whenever you can. It's a great learning tool to watch yourself, plus the process of preparing for a taping at a club helps you prepare for other tapings—like TV.

In terms of audio, sometimes you can plug into the soundboard, then have an additional mike that would pick up the room sound (laughter). The camera should be placed above the audience. And if it's high enough, you don't have to worry about the staff walking in front of the camera during a punch line—which they invariably do. In terms of clanking glasses, you can't control everything. Eliminate as many obstacles as you can. For example, don't place the camera near a table of drunk bachelorettes; make sure you're well lit and can be heard.

It took a lot of time to get my Letterman audition tape together. Even though the lighting and sound quality was better, I didn't want to send in stuff I'd done on TV. Plus, most of the material was new. I went around to lots of clubs taping and taping and taping. Sometimes the audience would be light, or not responsive, or I would be off. Sometimes the majority of the set would be good, but then a couple of the jokes wouldn't hit. I ended up making a compilation tape of sets from the Irvine Improv, The Ice House, and my one-woman show. Editing helped to keep the tape moving, lively . . . fresh. I knew that Letterman was intelligent and aware enough to understand that the tape was made in clubs and that as long as the sound was pretty good, that the material and my performance were more important than a flashy tape. I worked a lot with my dear friend George Miller, who watched all the tapes. When I finally had one that he felt was good enough, I sent it in. The tape, which was about eight minutes, got me the show!

FAQ 34 My Performance Wasn't Perfect—Can I Still Send Out the Tape?

What about sending out videotapes that are flawed? What I mean is that I have a good performance on tape that I'd like to send to bookers—but there's one moment where I look lost, like a deer in the headlights. —G.J.

What a coincidence—my wedding video has the same flaw. My "look" is always good for a few laughs every time we watch it, but I'd never send it to a booker because the entire production would be too expensive to take on the road.

Every comic is always searching for the "perfect" video that has great quality, while also showing him at his best on stage. He might think it can always be better (thus, the never-ending search), but if a booker can clearly see and hear the comedian is funny and gets a positive reaction from the audience, that's what counts in a world of imperfection.

Videos shot in clubs are not going to have the quality of a television production. Every experienced booker should know this, or they stand a good chance of missing out on many up-and-coming comedians—who might be inclined to return the rejection favor after making their network television debut.

Since we've already talked about the importance of visual and audio quality, what you need to do next is decide if your video is a good representation

of what you do on stage. Again, it won't be perfect and you'll always be looking to make a better one, but it can't be a "bomb" set either. If you're getting
laughs and look like you know what you're doing, it's probably acceptable and
should be used to get work.

When there's a moment in the tape (the "deer in the headlight look")
that you think definitely takes away from the rest of your performance, consider having it edited out. Someone with experience working a video editing
board should be able to do this very easily. If you happen to be in approximately the same position on stage before and after the section you want cut
out, the edit can almost be unnoticeable. If not, simply fade out the picture
right before that moment, then fade in afterwards. I've seen some very cool
effects where the comic will disappear in a bubble and reappear in another.
There's no rule that says you can't use your imagination when going for
a professional-looking video.

You never want to do too much editing, because bookers will wonder what
you're trying to hide. One edit can make it look like you were actually doing a
longer set, but cut it down to a more watchable time. Too many edits and it
might seem you're not being quite honest about the quality of the entire show.

If you're happy with the rest of the tape, don't let one moment ruin it.
A single edit is not a big deal, so cut it out.

Now, after taking a short break to laugh at my wedding video, it's time for
me to answer your original question. Should you send out a flawed video?
Well, not even my immediate family has copies of my nuptials . . .

If too many edits will earn you a reputation as a secret agent rather than a
comedian, you're risking the chance of looking unprofessional or inexperienced.
We know first impressions can mean a lot in this business, but success can also
depend on circumstances, timing, and hard work. There are comics who didn't
pass their first audition at a club and continued to return until they did. At the
former New York Improv, I remember comics who showcased six or seven times
before they were finally added to the roster. But in those cases, we were able to
see the dedication and growth in their performances. Eventually, the first impression was forgotten—unless we could dig it up for embarrassing reasons later.

Videotapes can be your chance to make a good first impression. The
reason you're probably sending it is because the booker is not located close
enough for an in-person showcase. His club or office may even be in your
backyard, but he would like to see a tape before putting you on stage in front
of paying customers. Your tape is your first impression.

If the first video doesn't get the desired results, it's perfectly acceptable to send a different one, usually about six months later to show you've taken time to work on your act. Hopefully (if you were turned down for work), the booker won't have a lasting, bad first impression. But if he does, you might be put on the back burner while they dig through a pile of tapes from acts they don't already have an opinion about.

Greg Giraldo

Nobody has a videotape that's perfect. But it really depends what you're talking about—for what purpose, for what reason, and what you're trying to get.

I don't send tapes anymore for club work or anything like that. Usually it's just for some corporate stuff. They have to clear the material and see that you can work clean for an extended period of time. So I send my half-hour Comedy Central tape or whatever.

If I was a young comic trying to get into a club and I had a tape, it would depend on what position in the show I was trying to get. If you have a tape with forty minutes of material that's all killer and you flub one line and you're looking to get a gig where you gotta do fifteen minutes, then I would say don't worry about the one flaw.

I don't think you'd want to have a tape that doesn't at least represent you well. If you bomb or something obvious, I wouldn't send it. But if you have a tape that you just think is not perfect because you forgot to do a bit or you sort of flubbed one thing, sure, don't worry about it.

But you have to be honest. Why is the tape not perfect? If it's not perfect because the material's not perfect, there's nothing you can do about that. But what is it that's wrong with the tape? I mean, if you have a tape where you're cursing up a storm and you're trying to get work in a sort of, you know, Christian club, if it existed, then that would not be a good tape.

FAQ 35 **Could You Give Me Some Hints about Being My Own Publicist?**

I won the semi-finals at an area comedy club contest. How should I use this success in contacting clubs and bookers? Do you think I should put that in my bio when I try to get other gigs and on my introduction for MCs to read? Should I send a note or postcard to the club manager? I didn't know if it was appropriate because it was for a contest, but it couldn't hurt, right? Should I wait to see how I do in the finals? —T.L.

Why wait for the finals? If you win that, a smart promoter (such as yourself) will consider it another (second) reason to get your name and credits out to people who can hire you. That's two promotional opportunities from one contest!

There's no better time to start promoting your current success than *right now*. Include your winning status in future stage introductions until it can be replaced by something more prestigious, or becomes embarrassingly outdated, which shouldn't be a problem if you believe "success breeds success."

Add this credit to your résumé under the heading Awards and find a way to work it into your bio. Any type of positive finish in a comedy contest means you've earned respect for your performance (by somebody, somewhere), and you need to get that information to people who can further your career.

If you've already contacted various bookers with a video and promo package, the best method to pass along information about career updates is by sending a postcard with the news and a note that you're available for work. You might also add extra importance by writing a press release (like the one that follows) and sending copies to industry people on your mailing list:

FOR IMMEDIATE RELEASE:

DATE: (Do this the morning after your achievement—why waste time?)

CONTACT: (Your phone, e-mail, and Web site address)

BINGO THE LAUGH MACHINE WINS COMEDY CONTEST!

Stand-Up Comedian, **Bingo The Laugh Machine**, won first place in the semi-final comedy contest held at Joe's House of Humor in Ocean Beach, Wisconsin. With a mix of gut-busting observational humor, song parodies, and a delivery that obviously impressed both the judges and audience, Bingo was declared the winner out of a competitive field of national comedians vying for this prestigious award.

Bingo is an up-and-coming stand-up comic who regularly performs at clubs throughout the area. A graduate of Mike's School of Hard Knock-Knock Jokes and a favorite phone-in guest on numerous morning radio shows (he makes the best song requests!), Bingo will be returning to Ocean Beach for the contest finals on (Day and

Date). Show time is 8 P.M. and tickets are $2 in advance and $3 day of show. For reservations and more information, call 555-5555.

For award-winning laughs, bookings, promotional package, interview, or more information, be sure to contact Bingo The Laugh Machine!

The above example could include more biographical information and a more accurate description of a comedian's performance style or topics. But since I invented Bingo The Laugh Machine (at least I hope there's not another!), there's an excellent chance you'll create something better working with the truth.

For bookers you haven't contacted, now's the time to do it with a promo package. Be sure to include your achievement in the cover letter because a success story always makes a great introduction—and first impression.

Any bookings or career highlights are great opportunities to stay in touch with bookers, clubs, agencies, and managers. Whenever you're basking in the glory of achievement, there's no better time than the present to let everyone know.

Jeff Abraham (Vice President, Jonas Public Relations)

Let me back up a second . . . It amazes me how many comedians you meet who do not have a bio or a decent head shot. Those are such basic tools. Everyone should have a great-looking head shot of himself that's recent—and a bio. And a bio doesn't have to be four pages starting with the day you were born, but it should be a good, simple one-page bio that has your credits and tells us what you're about. I would also include a résumé that lists the major clubs, TV credits, and things like that.

Then to continue with your question, a press release can be something that's a simple one-pager that's self-explanatory and tells me something about the performer. "Who" this person is and "why" someone would want to write about them. What distinguishes comic A from comic B. We should know something more about you after reading this press release, as well as about something upcoming.

When I usually send out a press release for a client, I send it to the local newspapers to let them know this comic is coming to the "blank club." So it has news in it. It's a "press release." It pertains to a current activity:

"So-and-so will now be performing at this club on these dates. Here's all the ticket information and everything the paper needs to know about the news." And then "Who is that performer?" Well, the performer is "This." He's done this—and this is who he is.

FAQ 36 How Far Can I Go to Make It a Show?

I'm interested in making my stage show more of an "event." It just doesn't seem enough to me, just standing in front of a microphone telling jokes. I've been told by too many comics that I have to make a decision about "who" I am on stage. They're probably right because I'm all over the place and maybe trying to do too much. But I also think if I have a talent for something, I should use it. I do stand-up, but also have props for magic tricks and do funny songs on my keyboard. If I ever get famous I can hire a road crew, but right now I'm dragging all this equipment to open mikes and auditions. I also get dirty looks because I need time to set all this up on stage. Would I be better off (and better accepted) if I just do jokes for now and plan more of a "show" after I make it? —T.B.

My back hurts just *thinking* about lugging a lot of heavy equipment around from one place to another. But you have given me an idea. When I "make it," I'm going to hire a road crew to carry a soft couch into my office and spend afternoons resting my mental back pain.

You can feel safe in the knowledge that you're not alone in your predicament. If performers didn't take chances at being different and exciting on stage, they'd all fit the category of, "Seen one—seen 'em all." That's not a goal to have when entering the comedy scene.

If you have a talent for something, it should definitely be considered for your act. If, of course, it's funny or can be made funny. Musicians, magicians, hypnotists, jugglers, and others with practiced talents are no strangers to comedy stages. I've seen trivia-buffs, spelling champs, English majors and comics who can name every state capital work their knowledge into hysterical bits. And using this talent not only offers ideas for material, but also can bring confidence in performing something on stage that you already do well.

Let me mentally lay down on my office couch and tell you a story . . .

A few years ago, I had a young college student in one of my workshops. During our first two meetings, he worked on a stand-up set that was acceptable for a beginner—meaning he could be confident doing open mikes. With experience and more writing, we all felt he would gradually improve as he continued.

After performing his act during our third session, it was obvious his confidence was lacking. The material just wasn't working up to his expectations. It was good, but lacked anything "different" than typical observational humor from a male college student. Then he made a half-hearted suggestion:

"I can do some impressions?"

"I don't see why not," I replied. "How many can you do?"

"Twenty-eight," he answered, stating the exact number.

When asked why he hadn't mentioned this talent before, he said it might be considered a "cheap laugh," and he wouldn't be taken seriously as a comic. He was also worried that too many other comedians already did impressions.

After agreeing there was a deluge of Robert De Niro and Al Pacino (both good and bad) on comedy stages, we also talked about the careers that impressionists such as Rich Little have maintained because of their talent. Then I asked whom he impersonated.

The answer was a list of contemporary comedians every college student and comedy fan would recognize—and definitely not over-done by others. Adam Sandler, Ray Romano, David Spade, and twenty-five more. With a little coaxing, he "did" each with a skilled talent for both vocal and physical traits.

To edit myself a bit here, the comedian, Eric Moneypenny, went on to incorporate this talent into a spelling bee routine and made a definite "impression" during our workshop showcase at The Improv. In addition to open-mike clubs, colleges welcomed his fresh attitude toward impressions, and he gained valuable experience with on-campus shows. Eventually, he found himself in Los Angeles auditioning for television—which should never be confused with cheap laughs.

When it comes to making your act a show, comedians have different opinions. To some, a show is telling jokes in front of a microphone. For others, it's using props, music, magic, or whatever best displays their talents. Bill Cosby sitting in a chair is as much of a show as Carrot Top filling a stage with his inventions. How much of a road crew you'll eventually need is your decision, based on talent, audience response, and possibly a strong back.

Since the voice of experience is always best, here are three examples of using your creative talent and making a show of it. Based on the success of each performer, I doubt anyone would ever use the term cheap laughs.

The Music Man: Weird Al Yankovic

Comparing comedy to music can sometimes be like the old apples-to-oranges theory. You remember that one, right? Both are good, but completely different. You can enjoy each in a variety of recipes, but not always together. For instance, apple/orange juice works, but you might skip dessert if both were the main ingredients in a casserole baked by a "weird" member of your family.

Sometimes (and I'm back to the comedy and music comparison here), the combination works great. After all, acts such as The Marx Brothers and Bob Hope always demonstrated their musical talents in movies, while everyone from Frank Sinatra to The Beatles had comedy films on their résumés. But they tended to keep the two forms separate. Harpo's renditions on the harp were still classical, while The Beatles sang the same lyrics to songs that made them pop music classics.

Occasionally an accident may happen that's not actually meant to combine the two, but still does. If you've ever heard William Shatner singing "Lucy in the Sky with Diamonds" you'll know what I'm talking about.

Putting comedy to music is nothing new and is what made musical satirists like Spike Jones and Allan Sherman famous years ago. Having a talent for both is still a great way to energize audiences. And when it's baked up by a "weird" member of the industry, it can be the basis for chart-topping singles and CDs, Grammy Awards or even honors from Rolling Stone Magazine and MTV. . . .

Weird Al

I started when I was, I don't know, fourteen or fifteen years old just doing stuff that I literally recorded in my bedroom on a cheesy little cassette tape recorder. Just me singing along with my accordion. Horrible, horrible songs! But I'd send them in to (radio host) Dr. Demento and he'd play them on the radio. Over the years I guess my material got better and I started building up a cult following. And at some point I decided, "Well, gee, I don't want to be an architect any more. I wanna be Weird Al for a living!"

When I first started out, the production wasn't anywhere nearly as big as it is these days, but it was still a rock 'n' roll concert none the less. And promoters didn't know how to handle us. They thought, "Well, you're a comedy act, so we'll book you in comedy clubs." And every once in awhile we'd be on a stage that was intended for, you know, a guy with a microphone and not a full-out rock 'n' roll band.

I remember we played this club in Nashville called Zanies. Nice club, but it's not a rock venue. The stage was so small that, literally, we could not move. We were placed tightly on the stage with the amplifiers out in the audience. I mean it was ridiculous! But we had a long talk with our agent saying, "You know, it's rock 'n' roll, so book us accordingly."

It's weird because I'm two mints in one. I'm both, but don't really fit neatly into either peg. I don't fit into either circle or world, because I'm not entirely accepted in comedy circles and [not] entirely accepted into music circles. I just feel like this guy on the fringe.

Wherever people wanted to see us, we'd go. What group of people really got behind us first? It was geriatric Japanese women! I don't know why . . .

No, not really. It's kind of an "all ages" show. The demographics kind of blow my mind because you look out at the audience and there's everybody from toddlers to grandparents. Probably, the hardest-core fans are teenaged and I probably do—and this is a broad generalization—but I tend to do probably better in the Midwest than in other places. But it really spans all the age groups and demographics.

Harry Anderson: A Magical Comedy Tour

A good magician never reveals his tricks. If he does, you can bet it's only a distraction while he's pulling off another that will leave you even more amazed. Conjure up a dose of laughter into the routine and—*poof*—a comedy-magician will appear.

Magicians can perform almost anywhere, from children's parties to the largest casino showrooms. Television specials are dedicated to sleight-of-hand tricks, mind-reading, and grand illusions. For high-paying corporate events, cruise ships, and colleges, magicians can work the audience on an intimate level with tabletop magic, then follow with big on-stage productions—while charging the client for both performances.

Is there nothing they can't do? Well, they can't play a comedy club unless they're funny.

A comedy-magician can be a bit of a con artist with a good sense of street-smart. He may seem like your best friend while stealing your watch, or the vision of evil as flames and sharp objects soar past a willing audience volunteer. Whether you're warned of what's coming or have the wool completely pulled over your eyes, it's easy to laugh when someone is "taken" with quick hands and funny material.

When magic and laughter are delivered in equal parts, a magician stands a good chance at finding work in the comedy business. It's all a matter of experience, confidence, and of course, talent. . . .

Harry Anderson

I've done it since I was eight years old; that's about when most guys who have an interest in magic take it up. It's about the age when you start thinking about hobbies, sports . . . So if you don't like playing outdoors and you can't juggle, you do card tricks.

Magic is either illusion driven or character driven. My show is a comedy show and it fits in a comedy club, but it's not solely comedy-magic. I do a lot of yappin' to the audience. And hopefully what you're going to do—and what a comic's going to do—is express a character to the audience. Because that's what they really want. The jokes are great, but it all has to add up to something where they get a feeling they've spent some time with somebody they could somewhat understand. If you do that, then television executives are the same as anyone else and that's how you end up acting on TV. You express a human being within the material and get a sense of a human being who is unique, as we all are. But we're not all able to express our uniqueness, and hopefully that's what the stand-up does at its best. I love good jokes, but any good joke teller can tell a good joke. It all adds up to a sense of character. I truly do think that's what we're interested in, whether it's soap operas or reality TV or whatever. What we're interested in is other people.

Harry the Hat was the character that got me my job. That got me my career. He's distinct. He's an individual and there's a lot of jokes and tricks that work for him. But underlying it, if you took that same material and gave it to an average comic, he wouldn't think it was that funny. And if you gave it to a magician, he couldn't pull it off. So I'm much more character driven than material driven.

I was a street performer, once I was fifteen. I was in high school in LA, went up to San Francisco for a summer and never looked back. My character developed on the street. My first work on the street was actual hustling. I was doing a shell game and playing gin on trains. I was kind of going along that way and then I got myself a broken jaw and a couple of nights in the stir. Then I decided to take a little different approach.

I'd acted in school and was always fascinated by it. So in doing the shell game, for example, rather than hustling for the twenty bucks, I'd do a comedy expose of how the game works—which came off as more of a magic trick. Then I'd collect a bunch of quarters instead. But my jaw was never broken after that!

But you know, it was fun! I was very lucky. I got to play in the street when there weren't a bunch of people living on the street and I got to play Vegas when the mob still owned the hotels. I got to do TV when there were still three channels. We didn't even have networks, they were just channels. So I kind of got to see the "golden age." I got to do The Tonight Show with Johnny! You know, that's the crème de la crème there.

My act is a little less physical now. I'm not shoving nails up my nose anymore or piercing my body with needles! But it's still all street based. It's still Three Card Monty, pick-pocketing, handcuffs, and money. At the end, I do a demonstration of card-counting that's kind of all blown out of proportion. Yeah, a little mental gymnastics. I've switched out of the physical gymnastics for the mental gymnastics.

There's nothing that happens that doesn't involve the audience. Because that's the nature of the beast. I mean, I have no interest standing on stage alone. It makes me too easy of a target! So I'm constantly getting somebody up there.

Robert Dubac: The One-Person Show

Let's face it. Most people tell stories and "do" characters. It just seems to be human nature. The overwhelming majority never do it on stage or write a character-based novel, but while delivering a story, they can take on various voice inflections, expressions, or movements for descriptive purposes.

If a child is teased to a point where he has to tell an adult, he'll often try to imitate the bully to make the offending lines sound real. If an employee is mocking his boss to co-workers or friends, he'll do a slight or over-exaggerated characterization to make it believable—and usually funnier. When someone is talking about their favorite episode of a sitcom, they'll almost instinctively deliver the best lines in the same vocal styles as the on-screen characters. It makes the story more "real" and entertaining enough to keep another person listening.

Comedians love doing characters and telling stories. It could be as simple as describing a conversation or thought, or overacting the story for comedic effect. Some may have enough on-stage characters to cast a sitcom, or have developed each to a point where different characters could do entire shows on their own. Others could have a wealth of material connected by a common theme that could be performed as a single piece with a beginning, middle, and end.

A stand-up comic on stage alone could be considered a "one-person show." But that's not what the term means in the entertainment industry. A one-person show takes the above elements—character(s) and material with a theme—and develops them into a theatrical production or play. The stage could still be in a comedy club, but the goal is usually a theater with staging, props, lighting, costumes, effects—and hopefully a curtain call following a performance containing a beginning, middle, and end.

Many comedians think about doing a one-person show as a creative outlet, a career goal, or to showcase their talents for television, movies or theater. But it's much more difficult than putting a couch on stage and performing their stand-up routine. There's a reason why most actors have training, writers re-write, and directors have jobs. It's called theater. . . .

Robert Dubac

A lot of my stand-up had relationship material in it. A lot of comics have that stuff, but I wanted to make it a little deeper. I started doing that in stand-up and it was kind of restricted. That's one reason why I tried to make it into a more developed thing.

I was fortunate because I had a pretty extensive acting background. I was doing stand-up just to make money between acting gigs. But it seemed the only acting roles I got would be the neighbor or the husband who was having the affair. All the film roles I got had that kind of an essence. They never wrote anything different, so I was kind of fed up with that.

I couldn't put the whole thing in my stand-up act. Just pieces of it. That's one reason why I think I was never that successful doing stand-up comedy, because I kept trying to do something different. I kept trying to tell a story and do character stuff. You know, they've got "setup, joke, take a drink. Setup, joke, take a drink. . . ." There's a certain cadence that you can't fool with in a comedy club.

It's a lot of hard work and a lot of discipline. It's putting on a different thinking cap too. When I write for doing just stand-up, it's "setup, punch line, setup, punch line." That's the way you're thinking and that's the way you write. But when you're doing stuff like this, you've got to add more elements to it.

I think that's what happens with a lot of comics. It's not that they can't handle it— it's just that they've never done it. So it's like, what elements to add or how to think?

Think visually and think more than "setup, joke." You have to think of a "payoff." It's a little bit of sitcom writing and a lot of theater writing. It all has to have extra elements added. There's a certain feel to it in a live theater and I think that's the way it should be presented to an audience.

Most stand-ups either didn't have that or didn't want the discipline of it. A lot of these guys are still comfortable doing what they're doing and they're not about to take four steps backward. Even if they do the same bit every night, they can shuffle the order or goof around. But with this, it's pretty much scripted. There's not a whole lot of room where you can say, "Well, I want to put this bit in before I do that bit and change it around because I can tell the audience is a little uneasy. Or I gotta go into the audience and then come back to my material." You can't do that with this kind of show. It's got a beginning, a middle, and an end. You start jumping around and it doesn't make sense.

When I first came in, most of the critics and theater people thought it was just a comic trying to do something "theater":

'Well, it's not really a play. It's mostly stand-up.'

It just depends. But when I reworked it and made it more applicable to the genre, I haven't had that kind of feedback.

It's interesting because I did the show in LA and a bunch of comics came. And they're all just dying to do something like this because they're just burned-out. They do corporate stuff and weeklong or weekend gigs in comedy clubs and they're just burned-out. They would just pray to do something like this.

So I told them they should get started on it. I'd like to see these guys out in the theaters, but it's gotta be a top-notch show. It can't be just a guy with furniture telling jokes. You've got to have a story and you've got to get it to another level. It's not that nobody's capable of doing it, they just haven't had the experience and they don't know in what direction to go.

It's succeeded beyond my wildest dreams because of the big places I tour through, around the country. It's obviously fulfilled something that people want to see. I think what I've realized is that a lot of people who don't normally go to the theater will come and see this type of show. And they're also burned-out from the normal, kind of tired stand-up comedy stuff, and they want to see something different.

I like the whole idea of doing a bunch of characters and telling a story with one person. I have a lot of time during the day, so I write and write. That's kind of what I'll do. When I'm in cities I'll stop into the clubs, try stuff out, and do different characters. What's really interesting though, is that I'll go into a lot of clubs nowadays and nobody knows who I am. A couple times I had to walk down the hall with whoever was running the club and show them pictures of me headlining the club ten years earlier. Since I headlined it then, maybe I could get on stage there again?

FAQ 37   How Can I Be Funny, When My Life Ain't Nothin' to Laugh About?

The bad news is that I got laid-off from my job. The good news is that I have an MC spot on Saturday. But I don't feel very funny—because I got laid-off. Do you have any suggestions on how to get back on track and work on my material? —M.W.

Hmmm . . . Let me get this straight. The American Dream has become The American Nightmare in the world of day-jobs, but you still have to be funny Saturday night. Okay, that is bad news and nothing to laugh about, but desperation (for lack of a better word) will often breed something to laugh *at.*

Hopefully, there are a few unemployment checks and another job in your immediate future, because the bottom line is to make ends meet and avoid poverty whenever possible. But if you're serious about having a career in comedy, that should be your ultimate goal.

I don't know what you do for a living or if it's the type of work that will allow time to perform as often as you'd like. Many comics look forward to a time when they can quit their "day job" and earn enough money doing comedy full-time. But until then, well, we all have to eat.

The job-hunting experience can bring a wealth of material. You may hate interviews, the unemployment line, and help-wanted ads, but keep your comic mind active during the process. The problem is more common than we'd like to think and is a subject many audience members will relate to. Use what little free time you have (because finding a job can often take more of your time than an actual job), and give your self-importance a boost by writing about the situation for your comedy act. Also remember that your next job might bring more material and eventually you'll make a voluntary exit to work on the comedy circuit.

The best thing to do immediately is to get on stage and let the audience allow you to feel funny again. Be honest with them if being laid-off is a problem and try to write material around that. Explain in your own words why it happened and why it happened to you instead of some jerk that might have deserved it more. Get it out of your system and do it with laughs, which is what a lot of great comedians have always done and will continue to do. After all, it's their job.

Christopher Titus

When I first started, I actually tried to be a comic—like "happy boy comic:"

"Hey, you ever notice that when you go to the store and you buy stuff and . . ."

I was gonna quit. I hated myself in comedy. But human beings are amazing

things. Eventually, your integrity will take over. You can only be a scumbag for so long. I was being a stand-up comic thinking that's what I had to do—appease them.

"Hey, you ever notice . . . ? Hey, blah, blah, blah . . . Don't you like me?"

Then one day I wrote a new piece that really had an edge to it. Actually, I was auditioning for Montreal [Comedy Festival]. This piece about fighting my dad and my mom in this mental hospital, but I was doing it, like, "Hey! Anybody's mom in a mental hospital?!"

I get off stage and my agent, Bruce Smith, goes, "What the fuck are you doing?!"

I was, like, shocked and went, "Whaaaat?"

He goes, "You're up there talking about your mom in a mental hospital and fist-fighting your dad and you're talking about it like you're Seinfeld. 'Hey, anybody notice that my mom shot a guy?'". . .

I was like, "The audience isn't gonna like me for what I really am. I'm kind of intense . . ."

And he said, "Look, man. They know you're lying to them. They don't know it on a conscious level, but that's why you don't kill like you should be killing."

So I went home that night and I wrote this bit called, "We Need Comedy to Get Rid of Our Desire to Kill." At the end of the bit I'm stabbing my boss in the chest with a letter opener and I'm screaming, "I just need a good laugh!" It's two and a half minutes long, and I went up at Igby's. I was so scared I took one of my buddies from acting class with me, because it was just a monologue. It was a ranting monologue about the worst day you could ever have and by the end of it you're stabbing your boss in the chest at his desk. And the audience went nuts! I finished this bit and they went, like, "YEAAAH!!"

Well, I didn't have anywhere to go. That was the only piece of material I had like that. I, like, freaked out. I was like, "So, hey, anybody ever go to the store and you buy a . . ."

And you know what? Here's what I learned about audiences. The audience stopped dead. I mean, I didn't get a laugh for the next seven minutes. I had two minutes—huge laughs, huge applause—the next seven minutes I ate it!

I went, oh man, they know when I'm lying to them. They saw me be who I really was and then they saw me lie to them. And they went, "Fuck you. We don't like you. If you're going to lie to us, we don't want to see you."

So from then on, I actually went home and I took my whole act apart. I actually got rid of . . . God, I threw away ten years worth of material. I just threw it away and then I started writing. That's really when I started writing about my mom killing her husband and I wrote about mental illness and I wrote about . . .

I actually went into my "pain vault," because I didn't realize how important it was or how much comedy was living in it. Then it just all came out. But I knew there was something funny in it and I kept digging and digging and digging, because it's a hard thing to go into. A lot of people don't want to hear it, but I found a way into it.

BACKSTAGE

FAQ 38 **Is it Professional to Get So Personal?**

I got a call from the owner of a comedy club that I performed in a few weeks ago. He left a message saying that he wants me to come over during the next show. He also said dinner and drinks are on him. He doesn't book the shows himself, so I don't know what to think. Does he want me to do a show, or is he inviting me for another reason? The message made me nervous for some reason. Do you have any idea what could be going on? —Ms. M.W.

I would suggest you start brushing up on a mentalist act. I've been amazed by a number of performers who claim to have ESP (many comedians have ESP*N*) and use psychic powers to entertain audiences with their amazing mental abilities. These talents can include reciting serial numbers on random dollar bills, naming siblings, children, pets, and why the IRS might question a company's entertainment tax deduction if they hire a mentalist for all board meetings.

I find these types of acts highly entertaining, even when they're done with or without comedy. But none have ever shared their trade secrets with me. If they did, I would be starring in lottery commercials and answering this while seated next to a swimming pool. Until then, I have no way to predict this club owner's true motives, but I can make a few guesses. . . .

One would be that he really enjoyed your act and wants you to grace his stage again. Comedians rely on return engagements and some look at dinner and cocktails as an added bonus—on top of their regular pay. But since he neglected to mention monetary compensation in trade for your comedy performance on his club's stage, I think we should stop trying to read his mind and get down to business.

The entertainment industry is a business. Like any business, there's always the chance of sexual harassment, discrimination, and other social roadblocks an employee or freelancer must sometimes contend with. It's a downside of human nature, but unfortunately it exists.

Did he act in a professional manner toward you while you were at his club? I refer to comedy as a serious business with a lot of laughs, and joking between management and performers can be a fun part of the experience. Humor often builds friendships and could be part of a business relationship resulting in more bookings. If a club owner dislikes you personally, his only reason for a repeat engagement is if you draw big audiences, resulting in more money for his bank account.

Even flirting can be a part of this. For some people, it's part of their human nature. But if this is leading someplace where you don't want to go, the best advice is to avoid it or demonstrate a few karate kicks during your act.

Since the bottom line is business, a certain amount of professionalism should be easy to detect. In between joking around there might be insightful conversations about the club, the audience, or your act. A good sign is if the owner pays you on time and shows more interest in his club, rather than throwing one-liners and come-ons to you.

You mentioned the owner wasn't the person who booked you into his club. If he personally scheduled all the performers, you would treat his message as a business call. Contact him and ask about your billing on the show and discuss your pay. This is a business and that's what you're interested in. If you're worried the conversation isn't going in that direction, tell him your calendar's full.

Since the original booking was through another person or an agency, contact the person you worked with. Explain that you received this message and you're calling about the job. Let them handle it and see what transpires.

Now, after shutting off ESPN and relying only on mental ability, here's my opinion. Don't go—unless you want to see him for any other reason besides comedy. Based on his phone call and your hesitation, it seems as if he has something other than business on his mind. Perhaps monkey business . . . ?

There's one question I ask all performers when a situation like this comes up. Unless a club owner or other contact admits they want to start booking acts and cut out the middleman, how did he get your phone number? There's no reason to give it to him since you were working through an agency. If you hope to avoid unwanted calls, it's something you must think about in the future.

Even without ESP, I know many performers put a home phone number and address on their promotional material. Of course promoters must have a way to contact you, but you never know who will end up having access to these essential business tools. This could lead to a situation more annoying than phone solicitors calling every night during dinner.

If you're serious about the comedy business and worry about uninvited calls, invest in an answering service. A human or machine (the good ones will sound like both), will be there 24-7 to take a message. This is an FAQ term meaning twenty-four hours a day, seven days a week, which gives you more time to write and promote yourself instead of waiting for the phone to ring. Check in with the service on a regular basis, return the messages you want, and discard the rest.

Only use this phone number on your promotional material. An address is not necessary because as a working comic, you're expected to travel from one end of the Earth to the other while furthering your career. If a talent booker thinks you're too far away, they may not call for a particular show. The choice should be yours as to whether you accept it or not.

Along with most everything else in this business, there are exceptions to my advice. If you are being mailed a check, you have to have an address. When that's the case, give them one when it's requested to confirm the booking. If you enjoy having an added buffer, rent a post office box and write it off as a business expense.

You might also develop a good relationship with your local clubs. Many comics have a "home club" where they got their start with lots of valuable stage time. Management knows they live in the area and can rely on them to fill last-minute cancellations or a regular spot without the added cost of a hotel room for the night. If it's to your advantage, let them know what nearby city, town, or suburb you're living in. Then stay prepared to make yourself appear—mentally and physically—at the right place at the right time.

Kathleen Madigan

Ever since I started, and this'll show you how old I am, I had a 1–800 voice-mail number. I don't think it's a good idea to give your home phone number out to anybody. Also, for business sake, I think it's unprofessional if a club owner is calling and it's your home answering machine. It just doesn't sound good. Now's there voice mail, but I would get a different number.

If a club owner is hitting on you, you set the boundaries. If they can't stay within them, then you may not be able to go back. I guess you could try to sue them, but realistically I can't see that happening. If he's that much of a jackass, then you probably wouldn't want to go back. I just wouldn't go back. That would be me, but that's also because I wouldn't spend, you know, $2,000 on a lawyer because this guy was hitting on me. I mean, I guess if he did something horrid I would, but if he's just hitting on me to the point where it's uncomfortable I would say something and then move on.

I wouldn't put any home stuff on those things. You can always go and get a voice mailbox for $19 a month, and it just looks better. It looks more professional when people are calling a voice mailbox, rather than somebody's answering machine: "Hey, me and my roommates aren't here . . ."

FAQ 39 **Where in Cyberspace Can I Find a Resource for Comedy Clubs?**

I'm hoping it won't be long before I join the ranks of working comics and can really start to garner some attention. I'm going to a different city for a few weeks on business and really want to do a show or two while I'm there. Except I'm really having a hard time finding any open-mike info for clubs in the area. If you could either do a little research or tell me what you know about anything relative to that, or point me in the right direction, I would be eternally grateful. Thanks a lot. —D.V.

It seems like everybody's on the move these days. One minute you're traveling down the comedy highway and—bam—you hit a roadblock. Clubs and open mikes that were thriving a year ago are gone, while the new jokesters in town are packing in audiences at a location that's nowhere on your map.

How do you find them? The best way is through the modern comedy information highway—the Internet.

In the late nineties, many comedians were still relying on various books and magazines to find clubs, open mikes, and booking contacts. For a yearly subscription rate you could receive a large book with all the required information and quarterly updates by mail. Another option was to buy monthly issues of different comedy-related magazines, hoping one would include the area in which you were interested. But these publications could be outdated before the ink is dry due to new clubs opening, old ones closing, or the listed booker, agent, or manager making a career change.

Today everything can be found on the Internet. Many clubs and agencies have their own Web sites with submission guidelines, while comedians use the technology to make their promotional material instantly available to anyone who needs it.

Innovative members of the comedy community have also dedicated cyberspace to help make your research easy. There are numerous comedy-related Web sites listing clubs and open mikes by countries, states, and cities, along with addresses and contact information. Some may even include club reviews and other helpful advice.

Most stops on this information highway are frequently updated by comics. If a club is no longer in existence or a new one has opened, the news is e-mailed and changes will be posted on the Web site. It's not 100 percent foolproof, but definitely better than relying on a book published last year.

The Internet is also full of message boards for comedians, and sites dedicated to the comedy scene in a particular area. If you're traveling to a city and interested in performing, log onto a search engine and, . . . well, start searching!

Now (after a brief comedic pause), you really didn't think I'd leave you hanging like that—did you? I actually did a little research and here are some results that will help you get started.

I run a free comedy information service creatively titled The Comic "Spam" List to share updates about performance opportunities. At last count there were over five hundred comedians on the list from all parts of the world who receive these notices by e-mail. If you're interested in exactly what it's about, visit *www.thecomedybook.com*.

In the name of research, I asked members of the list to suggest the sites most helpful in finding clubs and open mikes. The results are in and here's what they said:

The Comic "Spam" List

www.chucklemonkey.com
www.comedysoapbox.com
www.employnow.com/comics.htm
www.heylady.com
http://members.aol.com/bookerlist/comlist.html
www.roadcomics.com
www.sheckymagazine.com
www.twelveteenmagazine.com

FAQ 40 Is an Audition a Good Place to Try New Material?

I'm going to Chicago to audition for a comedy festival. I'm really psyched about this, but don't know why. It's not that I think I'm ready to win something that big right now, but at this point just being in the game is a thrill. It's like buying a lottery ticket, I guess.

I have some new material that I'm anxious to use, but haven't done it on stage yet. Is that a smart thing to do? Or should I use the old reliable bits? —G.J.

I hate to give away my age, but here's a hint. Since all the music I grew up with is only heard on Classic Rock radio stations, you can guess I'm not a teenager anymore. And when I pay big bucks to see one of these musicians in concert, I expect to hear the songs that made them famous. If they haven't had a hit in twenty years and announce something from their latest CD, you can see the hoards of baby-boomers rushing for a bathroom break, then hurry back to their seats when they hear the opening chords of a song they recognize.

This is a good way to look at any audition or showcase. Present to them your best material. In other words, material that you've had the most success with and most likely got you into the position to get that showcase.

Let's say your favorite singer is Pat Boone (hint: I'm not *that* old!), and think of the hundreds of songs he's recorded. Much to your astonishment, you run into someone who has no idea who Pat Boone is. If your goal was to make that person a fan, what album would you have them listen to first?

My guess is you'd put his "Greatest Hits" collection on the turntable (yeah, I'm *that* old!), which would include only a fraction of his songs. But they would be the ones that made him famous and earned your everlasting admiration. What you probably wouldn't do to make this person a Pat Boone fan is play an album with songs even you had never heard before. If there wasn't a potential toe tapper in the bunch, you could end up looking pretty silly wearing white bucks and snapping your fingers to tunes that would send a hoard of baby boomers rushing for a bathroom break.

When you're doing an important showcase, go with material that has been proven to work in front of an audience. The idea is to perform your "Greatest Hits" and earn enough admiration to get the gig.

Too many comedians have learned that lesson the hard way. They'll write something new they think is great, but hasn't yet been tested in front of an audience. They might get on stage and discover a number of flaws in the material that could've easily been fixed by performing it a few times before the showcase.

For example, a comedian may assume the audience knows too much or too little about a certain subject that is a key element to their performance. In one of my workshops, a teenaged guy was doing a very funny routine about professional wrestling. When I noticed there were a few people in the room who were not laughing, I stopped him in mid-sentence and presented a simple question that would help explain to everyone else what he was talking about.

I asked if there was anyone who didn't know what the initials "WCW" stood for. A few people (the ones who weren't laughing) raised their hands.

When the comic explained it referred to World Championship Wrestling, they understood what he was talking about. Of course he couldn't believe anyone wouldn't be familiar with a topic he found so interesting, but learned through experience the possibility of performing to a crowd that didn't know Hulk Hogan from The Incredible Hulk.

There's also a chance the opposite could happen. When inexperienced comics are working on new material, they sometimes go into long explanations with too many details that are unnecessary and take valuable time away from being funny. One workshop example occurred when a college student gave a long dissertation about where his school was located, the size, what degree he was going for, how many years he had left, and the mascot's name—before getting into a story that we could laugh at.

I told him the extracurricular effort might get him a good job in the college admissions department, but the workshop members were breaking up into small discussion groups and comparing SAT scores. In his particular case, all he needed as an opening to the bit was to tell us he's a college student—then get into what is funny about it. If he attends an area school, he could mention the name to see if anyone in the audience had gone there. That might help in making a connection with those audience members, while it's safe to assume the others have probably heard of it. If he wants to give directions on where it is, do it in the parking lot after the show—unless the information is a key element to the routine.

The idea is to work out any problems in the material before using it during an important showcase that can further your career. This is a reason why great and experienced comics such as George Carlin and Jeff Foxworthy go on the road to test material before taping one of their television specials. They want the best guarantee that the material works before it's broadcast to millions of people who can voice their opinions with the power button on a remote control.

This also explains why many television shows employ a staff of writers. The idea is to bounce ideas off each other, like a comedian does with an audience when working out new material. The finished script will have gone through numerous rewrites, each time eliminating and adding material until the staff feels it has a good chance of being accepted by the show's viewers. If the material doesn't work they might not have a job next season, which is how a comedian should look at an important showcase.

Take the guesswork out of your showcase and prove to the bookers you have experience at making an audience laugh. After you pass the audition and get the job, you won't have to wait until next season to use their stage while adding in the new material to your act.

Barry Katz (Producer)

You have to come to play with your A Game—always. The only exception would be if your act is a "Throw Caution to the Wind" kind of act—like early Gilbert Gottfried, Bob Goldthwait, or Andy Kaufman—which was their signature and made them special to the industry. Otherwise, preparation and tried-and-true prepared material is the best way to go.

Three Auditioners Walk Into A Bar

- **Showcase Club.** These clubs are mostly found in New York and Los Angeles. Larger booking agencies throughout the country will also use one of their clubs for the same purpose—which is to see new talent. This is where a comedian will audition with a short performance that could be for a number of different reasons. These can range from simply being added to the club's talent roster, for out of town bookings, gaining representation, or consideration for a television appearance.

- **Agency Showcase.** When a comedian is signed with an agency or manager, the representative will schedule a block of time during a show when only a selection of their clients will perform. They will promote and invite members of the industry who could offer these clients work that will further their careers.

- **Television Showcase.** When a television show is looking to book comedians for an appearance, they will schedule a block of time at a club. This is normally done in the evening during a club's regular show—in front of a live, unsuspecting audience. The producers of the program might have certain acts they're already interested in, or rely on different agencies, managers, or the club's talent coordinator for recommendations. These performances are usually very short, often ranging in time from just three to five minutes.

Bobcat Goldthwait

You know what's weird is that I know a lot of guys have these steps put in their head. It's like when I was twenty, I'd just call and get, like, an assistant. And I'd say, "Hi, I'm a comedian. My name's Bobcat Goldthwait and I'd like to audition for the show." I was that naïve. But I think that a lot of people have set up these, like, things in their brain that, you know, "I 'have' to get to Montreal [Comedy Festival] before I . . ." You know, all this stuff. Man, I think you just do it.

But you know what I think the biggest thing is—and I certainly was the king of it—is you can't make these people the enemy. You know what I mean? I would go on stage and would have a good set, and then at the end of the set I would self destruct and tell people to go fuck off. The people I was auditioning for. And I certainly didn't corner the market on that. I've seen so many guys who do that.

It's really scary and you've got a big ego that you're already an established comedian. That 'people like me. People come out to see me,' or whatever. Or 'I do well and I've done well in this room.' Then you go up there and tell them to go fuck off. It's so crazy because the last thing is, when you're struggling to get on stage at an open mike . . .

I mean, I did anything. I kissed ass and I hung out with a lot of people I didn't, you know, like, just to get that three to five minutes on stage. And I'd go up there and like I said, I'd have a good set and then I'd make some joke about their network or their TV show or whatever. All the comics would laugh and I'd be, like, considered edgy for doing it. But in the meantime would blow some really nice, sweet gigs.

Don't go up there with an attitude of, How dare you hire me? If you genuinely don't want to be on something or you think it is cheesy, then don't do the showcase. You know what I mean? No reason to make these people think you're an asshole. It is sooo high school. I'm still banging into people that I forgot I even pissed off.

FAQ 41 Will Making Friends and Networking Really Help Me Book Gigs?

I just opened for a headlining comedian who said he really likes my act. He thought it complimented his style (we both work clean) and worked as a good warm-up for the type of audiences that come to see him. We also got along really great and the entire weekend has to be the highlight of my brief career.

He talked about requesting me to be his opener whenever he's in this area and maybe work some shows together on the road. Can headlining comedians do this? Would he be considered my agent? (In other words, would I have to pay him a commission?) —M.B.

Yes and no. It depends. Let me try to explain. . . .

Of course there are headliners who have more clout than others. Sometimes it depends on the specific market. If a club owner has been salivating for years to book a certain headliner because it's a guaranteed full house and he stands to make a lot of money, then the headliner can call a few shots in the deal. This might include a first-class hotel, limo service to the club, and even a request for his opening acts.

Other times the headliner might assume a little too much self-importance and make certain demands. The owner could say, 'Take it or leave it—along with the opening acts I've already booked.' Then a decision has to be made. If the headliner needs the show, you might have to wait until his star shines a little brighter to latch on.

Still, this is a good way to get bookings. If you've impressed someone who has influence to get you work—whether they're a headliner, booker, agent, or even a friend of a friend who owns a club—that's what you're trying to accomplish in this business. It's the basic reason behind sending out promotional material, showcasing, and making connections. It's called networking.

Is this headlining comedian who gets you work your agent? No. You do not owe him a commission. Buying dinner or a thank you gift is not out of line, but from what you describe, this is a personal and professional favor that is the result of successful networking.

Of course there's always the chance of other circumstances. If the headliner says he's acting as your agent and expects a commission for the booking, then you have to make a decision if it's worthwhile to enter into this business deal. If he demands a commission for all future bookings at the same club—regardless of whether he's headlining—then tell him to make the trip alone. When it's time for you to have an agent, find one who does it for a living and not someone who expects you to pay for the ride on their coattails.

Ellen Cleghorne

I don't watch Survivor *regularly, but stand-up is much like that show. You have to form powerful alliances if you want to succeed in this business.*

Take, for instance, Kings of Comedy. *Four men doing a show together that got them all national and international recognition.* Kings of Comedy *wouldn't have sold one-eighth the DVDs. Strong alliances.* The Blue Collar Tour *with Foxworthy, etc . . . Strong alliances. Even though stand-up might look like something you do alone, it's not. You have to have partners.*

Be friendly with everyone. Dress nice, whatever that means to you. Smile—you're a comic! Shake a hand and make a friend.

FAQ 42 Is Laughter the Best Medicine?

I'm a biology teacher. I think my main purpose as a teacher is to "edutain" students, which saves us a lot of money in toothpicks since we're more likely to keep our own eyelids open. I'm considering teaching a unit on the biological effects of humor in humans, which will conclude with students doing an original stand-up routine. Are many comics aware of the health values in humor and laughter? Would you have any suggestions or ideas for me to help get this off the ground? Thanks —M.M.

Where were you when I had to take a biology class in school? Our main assignment was dissecting a frog, and being somewhat squeamish, I never found any humor in it. But to get our required daily laugh, a few of us smuggled parts of our frog into the cafeteria on a day when they were serving soup and . . .

I'll stop there because I don't need any more marks on my permanent record. But to say the least, some of us are still laughing about it.

Your suggestion is a very good idea for a class, especially with all the current studies about the healthy value of humor. When I talk with groups of high school and college students, it's very clear that an entertaining teacher, usually with a sense of humor, makes attending class a lot easier. Chances are also pretty high that the students will learn more in the process—just by showing up.

Think back to a class you might have found boring and add an instructor with zero personality and . . . Well, who would want to remember anyway?

The same holds true in the business world. I'm sure employees would gladly produce more for a boss they enjoy working with, rather than a grouch who doesn't smile unless he's firing someone.

What makes these studies on humor even more exciting is that members of the medical community are looking into the results and incorporating humor into their bedside manner. This is why it's not uncommon to see comedians, variety acts, and clowns entertaining in hospitals, rest homes, and different medical facilities.

"A smile is better than a frown" complements "An apple a day keeps the doctor away" for a very valid reason. It's good for you.

Whether it's biological or simply a theory, if laughter can help someone feel better—even for only a moment—then it's worth using. In the best scenario, it may aid in recovery by stirring emotions about the better things in life. Or it might just bring a smile and a short, but valuable mental recess from the daily stress.

A very good organization to contact is the Association for Applied and Therapeutic Humor (AATH). Their membership covers a wide range of people from doctors, nurses, and researchers, to lawyers, teachers, writers, stand-up comics, lecturers, and clowns. A great representative for this style of medical procedure is Dr. "Patch" Adams, who is the real-life subject of the popular movie starring Robin Williams.

The basic theory is that laughter is not a cure-all, *but* it doesn't hurt. There's also proof it actually helps, most often as a stress release for both patients and their families. There have been studies showing the brain reacts in a positive and healthy manner when it hears the punch line to a joke, but this is where I must stop. After all, I'm not a scientist—unless you count a biology class frog and a bowl of soup as an experiment.

For more information about the healthy value of humor, I suggest you contact AATH. As of this printing, they can be found online at *www.aath.org*.

Jonathan Katz

My feelings about the health effects of humor? I know that comedy has a healing effect on people, but that's not a good reason to go into comedy unless you can't get into medical school.

If making someone laugh also makes them feel better, that's great. But don't let it distract you. Sometimes in comedy, you can make people nauseous and that's not always a bad thing. If comedy is what you're doing, you just want to make them laugh.

On a more personal note, I have fainted three times in my life from laughing too hard. And that's true. Two times were laughing at something John Benjamin said to me, the guy who played Ben in the series Dr. Katz: Professional Therapist. *Then a friend of mine found out, who's a nurse, that even though she's made me do spit-out coffee, she's never made me faint. She's very competitive, so one night she made me faint.*

We were at a restaurant in Boston and my wife said to her, "Nancy, shouldn't we be worried? He seems to have lost consciousness." And she said, "That's just your body's way of telling you that you need to breathe." She was so calm about it. It was amazing.

You know how when you're a little kid and someone's tickling you and you can't catch your breath? I couldn't. She's just very witty. It was a combination of drinking red wine and a well-timed joke. You can't just be witty. It has a lot to do with timing and you have to be sort of consistently witty. So there are biological effects to humor.

For reasons unknown to me, I used to carry a doctor's bag. Before I was even in comedy. I had a ping-pong racket in there. I was a serious ping-pong player. But having that doctor's bag on a bus in Manhattan, if somebody faints it's useless. Being funny if somebody faints is useless also. Now that's a long boring story for you.

FAQ 43 I Know You Can Help Me, but How Much Are You Gonna Pay?

I got a call from a club owner who said he's looking to break in new comedians for MC and feature spots. I asked how much the spots paid—and he got insulted! He said it was just an opportunity to perform and I should thank him for offering it to me.

I need the stage time, but I also feel I've worked long enough for free. I know he'll make money off the customers. Was I wrong for asking? —R.P.

When you're dealing with money, there are two sides to every coin. In the comedy business, there are two sides to every show: the booker and the performer. One can't exist without the other—and that holds true even if the same person is doing both jobs.

When a new comedian is looking for stage time, free performances at open-mike rooms are necessary and worthwhile for the experience in front of an audience. The club owner can offer this opportunity if the business is financially successful by earning money from cover charges, drinks, and food. Again, both sides of the coin should be happy.

Once a comedian reaches his goal of being a paid act, he can begin to consider finances as a factor in where he chooses to perform. Basically, he can accept or reject the offer depending on if he feels the payment is worth the effort.

This is especially true when a comedian is a headline or feature act working on a regular basis in the better-paying clubs. My feeling is if someone is still looking for MC or feature work in smaller clubs, money shouldn't be the main consideration. If the fact is that he can't afford to perform there because of travel costs or other expense-related reasons, then he shouldn't go. The finances will decide that option. But if it's a show that can be done with an acceptable amount of sacrifice (driving across country for a one-night gig is an accepted option for the very dedicated), then he should be more concerned about getting stage time, making connections within the industry, and adding credits to his résumé.

On the other side of the coin, comedians will undoubtedly begin to wonder how much the booker is earning as opposed to what the comics are being paid. If they begin to notice the club is successful solely because of the comedy shows, they have the right not to perform unless fairly compensated. In that case, the two sides can't exist together without resentment and are better off working out an acceptable financial agreement or looking for new partners.

How much comedians are paid depends on the venue, the status of the performer and booker within the industry, and the amount each side thinks the other is worth. The star of a hit sitcom is more likely to play a theater rather than a comedy club and have either a set price or a deal in which he receives an agreed amount per ticket sold. This last option is called a "door deal" and some of the more popular club headliners will also negotiate this type of an arrangement, along with a guaranteed minimum salary to assure it makes their effort worthwhile in case there aren't as many people in the audience as expected.

Quite often in those door-deal cases, you'll see the comedians doing more newspaper, television, and radio interviews than normal to promote their upcoming shows. The effort is made to bring in larger audiences so they can make more money. Some performers might even stand in the back of a club and count the paying customers to get an idea of how much they should be earning.

For the acts who've yet to hit the financial benefits of the comedy lottery, they'll probably have to agree to perform for a club's standard payment. This amount varies widely depending on how prestigious the club is—and can also work for or against the performer.

For instance, a certain club may have a great reputation as a place to be "seen" by industry people. Or, maybe it has a desirable location, great audiences, comfortable accommodations, good food, or it's a clean place as opposed to a dump. Whatever the reason, let's assume it's a club at which you want to perform very much. This situation could give a booker the upper hand in financial dealings and he may pay less than other, less desirable clubs. If he chooses to have you perform there, it's your decision whether the extra benefits are worthwhile.

Many comedians who are new to the business have asked me to give the exact dollar amounts they should be earning per performance. This is almost impossible to do in general terms because of the wide variety of clubs and the comic's status within the industry. But based on some of the figures I've encountered over the years, I'll make a rough estimate.

First of all, if you're new to the comedy business, don't plan on quitting your day job. It will probably cost you more in gas, food, and lodging than you'll earn during the early days of your tour through the comedy trenches. If you're lucky and end up with a few extra dollars, invest it in your promotional material and don't be late for work in the morning.

To make a purely educated guess, MCs can earn anywhere from a free meal for one show to approximately $300 for a six-night engagement in a full-time comedy club. As you might guess, there are a lot of potential figures within that range. An acceptable amount is $50 per show—but again, it depends on the club and how worthwhile it is for the performer. If you look at the $300 payment as being more desirable, you might be surprised to learn that figure is based on nine shows (including two Fridays and three Saturdays), which works out to roughly $33.33 per performance. What you need to consider is that it's steady employment for a week and worth the comedy effort.

The feature act should make more than the MC because he'll be required to do more time on stage. And in the effort of fair employment practices, he should also have more experience and be considered a funnier act, which is how bookers decide who should be in what position. On a regular comedy circuit and assuming the MC is getting $50 per show, the feature could earn anywhere from $75 to $150 for each performance. During a six-night engagement, $500 to $700 is not unheard of, but once again it depends on the club.

A headliner will do the most time on stage and be paid more than the other acts. If we were to base this on an MC earning $50 and a feature earning $100, the headliner's pay would be in the $200 neighborhood. A six-night stand might start at $1,000 and go up depending on the star act's drawing power and reputation.

I want to once again make it very clear that these are only estimates based on what I've learned from both bookers and comedians. Earnings were generally higher during "The Comedy Boom" of the mid-eighties to early nineties, when a six-night stand could be worth $500 to an MC, $750 to $1,000 for a feature, and $1,200 on up for a headliner. The comedy club market then went through a downsizing period, which affected the pay scale for many. In the past few years the industry has been making an upswing with new clubs and familiar chains expanding. Bigger audiences translate into bigger paychecks—for both sides of the coin.

Payment in showcase clubs, the corporate, college, and cruise ship markets, as well as any special events that would include private parties, festivals, or opening concerts for name performers all have different payment rates. A headline performer doing a shorter set in a showcase club might earn only $10 to $20 on a weeknight. Corporate event planners may not even blink an eye to pay a comedian $10,000 and up for a single performance. As always, it depends on the individual comedian's name recognition and status within the industry.

Brian Heffron (President, Heffron Talent International)

There is no doubt comedy is on the upswing, for two reasons. One, all the shady clubs kind of went away in the nineties and the cream rose to the top. And I think what's happening is club owners are really putting on a great product in terms of service, accessibility, great food, and creating an environment to let these guys work in, which is much more comfortable than it was.

Number two is, and this is my own personal opinion, there seems to be a wealth of tremendous talent that has come out in the last few years. It's a buyer's market right now, as far as I'm concerned.

Comics are making way more than in The Comedy Boom. I've always paid a lot for the best talent around, and I'm paying at least a third more than I was five years ago. That's not for the MCs, but just the guys who are selling tickets. In terms of pay grade, the MCs are getting about the same as five years ago.

FAQ 44 How Far Do I Gotta Travel to Get Booked in My Local Club?

It's amazing to me that I can get booked for a week in Las Vegas, but I can't get into one of my local clubs to save my damn life (sorry, just a little bitter). The whole "playing the game" is a pain, but I'm trying. For the life of me, I can't get booked near where I live. I've toyed a couple of times with the idea of changing my name and claiming that I'm from New York since I have a bit of the NYC edge to some of my material. What do you think about that—or should I keep on keeping on? —T.W.

Even New York can be a bitter town, especially for a comedian who is not on his neighborhood comedy club's A-list. Without hurting my brain too much, let me try to explain how I think you're feeling.

Bitterness is a cynical attitude fed by anger, frustration, or simple displeasure over situations that are important to the comedian, fueled by any feelings of personal rejection. It can also provide an unending source of humor, which is why some performers will incorporate the trait into their delivery. This style is often credited with giving an "edge" to the comedy, which is a recognizable New York State of Mind both inside and out of the Big Apple city limits.

Excuse me while I take a couple of aspirin after that dissertation. . . . In your case, and in many others, no apology is ever needed for your comedic tone. If you're mad about your current situation, using the attitude in your on-stage delivery can give you what is popularly known as that New York edge. Bitterness can make your on-stage persona interesting, sinister, or ultra-cool, but if in reality you think the subway is only a sandwich, there might be more than a few comedic bullets aimed in your direction if you start claiming to be from The City That Never Sleeps.

Quite a few very good comics complain about not being able to get bookings at clubs that are close to where they live. One reason is that the bookers look at them as being "local," which is a type of comedy discrimination that can rear its ugly head when comparing you to an act from a strange and exciting place such as New York, Hollywood—or any place they can't find in a road atlas.

Bookers can have the bad habit of sometimes viewing local comics as not much more than open-mike acts. This could be a hangover from a bad first impression if the comedian had showcased at their club when he wasn't ready to be considered a professional. He might also have performed during numerous amateur shows at the club, or is so regular on the local open-mike scene that the booker doesn't see any reason to pay when he usually works for free. And unless by some remote chance they're in the audience at a different club on a night when the comic is having a great set as a paid performer, it could be difficult for them to change their opinion.

Even if the comedian has a long list of respectable credits, the booker might wonder why he's still in the area. This thought process would follow the line that if he were truly good, he would have moved up the comedy ladder by relocating to New York, Hollywood, or another strange and exciting place somewhere in the road atlas. Of course we know this is a small-minded way to look at the comedy world, but it's also the nature of the industry outside of cities with numerous comedy and showcase clubs. To put it in business terms, why should they start paying for an act that area audiences have already seen— probably for free?

A good reason would be that the comedian is funny. Another would be experience and the ability to do a great job on stage.

As a comedian, the goal is to find an opportunity to prove you're more than ready to be considered as a paid act. If you can back-up that claim, then save the money it will cost to maintain a New York phone number, mailing address, and all the other expenses needed to "prove" you're strange and exciting enough to play their club.

Assuming you have an act that should be successful in front of their audiences and experience at similar clubs outside of the area, it's time to look at the contacts you've made. The best resources are comedians you've worked with in the past, have a good relationship with, and are currently getting work at your local club. When they're playing in your area, ask them to give you a great recommendation and continue to follow up on it. Since the booker hired the comic, he should have some respect for his opinion and you might eventually get an opportunity to showcase.

If you don't have this type of valuable connection, then you'll have to rely on another version of "playing the game." Submit your promotional material and/or make personal contact with the club booker. Explain that you live in the area and would like to be considered a very reliable option in case a scheduled act cancels at the last minute. You can be available to take their place on short notice and whenever the need arises, the booker can count on you. Send postcards or your avails on a regular basis, and then be ready when the phone rings.

I've seen this happen so many times that it shouldn't be written off as wishful thinking on my part. For whatever reasons, a booker will occasionally find himself in a situation where he needs a comic immediately. That's when his phone book comes out and frantic calls are made for a replacement. If you've done your homework and stayed in touch about being "willing to help," you'll stand a better chance of getting on stage than sulking in quiet bitterness over being ignored in your own backyard.

Once you establish yourself at your local club, most likely as an MC at first, this same technique can be applied for feature and headline work. Many clubs can only afford the top-name comedians on their busiest nights, which are normally the weekends. Rather than paying additional expenses to bring in someone else from a more strange and exciting location, the booker will find a comic in the area to fill out the week's schedule. There are a number of comics who take advantage of this situation and at the end of the year they often find they've performed more dates at their local club than they would have if they were only trying for strictly one-week engagements.

Finally, if you really feel your location does nothing to help you gain respect, leave your address off any promotional material, and use a toll-free phone number for bookers to contact you. Many lecturers do this to give them a more "worldly" image—even if they're only walking from next door to collect a check.

Maryellen Hooper

People ask me [about how difficult it can be to get bookings at your local club] all the time and I tell them that's been true from day one. And I think it will be true until the end of time. I think it's because when you are starting out, you do your open-mike nights, and they can't forget you with that picture of you with that lampshade on your head. Which, you know, is how dumb we all are in the beginning and how awful we are.

I actually went back to my home club and did a guest spot. I did a ten minute guest spot in the middle of the show, got a standing ovation, and one of the waitstaff told me they were writing in on comment cards, "When are you going to have her back?!"

So I called after a couple of days for my feedback. They said "Naw, you're still a little raw. Still a little green." You know, they just can't get over it.

That's why I moved so much. Every time I moved from one city to the next, I moved up on the ladder. Okay, I'm in New York and I'm a regular on open-mike nights. Now I move to Philly—I'm an MC. I moved up to New Jersey and I was a feature. I moved out to LA—I'm a headliner!!

I think it's just a fact of the business. Unless you buy the club owner dinner or have pictures of him in the nude in an uncompromising position, then [getting regular bookings at your local club is] not gonna happen.

FAQ 45 Can I Get My Big Break on Local TV?

Is doing comedy for a local television station good or a waste of time? —C.L.

It depends. The average person—as opposed to the not-so-average person (like a comedian), who has some experience pursuing a career in show business, tends to place celebrity status on almost anyone who appears on television. Even the guy interviewed on the evening news about his alien abduction will gain a little notoriety—at least around the trailer park ('Ya sure looked good on TV last night, Jim-Bob!'). So if the hints that your family or friends are dropping—about a comedy career being a waste of time—are as subtle as an Acme Anvil aimed at Road Runner (sorry, I have kids and watch too many cartoons), then an appearance on local TV might have these critics asking for your autograph.

A dedicated comedian can look at almost any opportunity for stage time as being worthwhile. Except we both know that's not necessarily true. (Those 4:00 AM shows in front of three drunk customers are pretty worthless, even if one or two of them are still awake. An optimist will at least consider it an opportunity to do his routine out loud, while an entrepreneur might think about making a few bucks by calling himself a designated driver and charging by the mile.)

It's important to consider the type of television show and the viewers it attracts. Local shows in major markets, such as New York and Los Angeles, have the potential for huge audiences, but if it's geared for bird-watching enthusiasts in a foreign-speaking community, chances are it won't help increase your fan base or lead to many job offers. If the show is somewhat popular in your area and is professionally produced, there's no reason not to take advantage of the experience. Most cities have their own "Morning Show" (or afternoon if it's a place where people tend to sleep late), with local hosts highlighting local people or events. This is a good way to promote upcoming shows or your career in general. In fact, some clubs make these appearances mandatory for headlining comedians, which can be more tiring than their actual performance and a good excuse to sleep all afternoon following early morning treks through local TV and radio studios.

When it's done on a much smaller level, such as a local cable channel with a broadcast signal that couldn't power a small flashlight, then you might have to decide if it's worth the effort. Here are three possibilities you should look into:

1. Will there be a live audience? Often in the world of cable television, there won't be anyone to laugh at your material other than the host, a camera-man, and a technician behind a soundproof glass, who are all more involved in the production of the show rather than in what you're saying. If that's the case, then the next question may not carry as much weight. . . .

2. Will you get a video copy of your appearance? It's very rare when you can't, but it would be best if the resulting tape continues your growth as a comedian. It always helps in the learning process to observe how you appear on stage and your performance techniques. But without a studio audience, the only crowd response will come from your imag-ination. That's not a problem if you have a big ego, but for an honest opinion it's important to hear the laughs. Even if it's a great quality video, it's wise not to send it out for promotional purposes without an audience reaction.

3. The experience. If your goal is to someday appear on the best television shows, then it's wise to already have a general idea of what it's like to do your set in front of a camera in a studio, rather than on a typical comedy club stage. You may still freeze when Leno or Letterman announces your name, but at least the sight of a camera won't cause you to forget your first line.

Basically, your appearance on local television should depend on the reputa-tion and your opinion of the show. If it's an amateur production with hardly any viewers or respect, you're probably better off spending your time doing club dates. But if it's one of those underground, on-the-edge and hip (how old am I?) shows and your act happens to fit the programming style, it might make an inter-esting short segment within your promotional video while also giving you some exposure to a new audience.

Another consideration for local television is if you are one of the main forces behind the show. You may have an idea for an original program, but not a winning lottery ticket to produce it or buy the type of friends who could. In that scenario, you start small and aim for the big time. Eventually you might become a local celebrity, host regular shows at area clubs, gain experience and confidence to move on to more successful projects and . . . Well, Phil Donahue started with a local television show and wound up marrying Marlo Thomas—so you do the math.

Dave Attell

Well, what's another choice? Ha! I think anytime you get a chance to do television, you should do it—outside of gay porn. There was a show in New York called Dave Juskow & Friends *that I did some stuff on. We're talking about cable access. You should talk to Juskow about it, because he has all those great stories. . . .*

Dave Juskow (writer and filmmaker)

There's local television, like an affiliate for NBC, and local public access. There's a big difference. If we're talking about public access, I still don't think you can waste your time if you're putting yourself out there. However, public access has certainly changed. It's not the same as it used to be, at least here in Manhattan. This is my favorite thing because it always makes you feel old when you have to start, "You see, back then . . ."

Well, back then, seriously, you know how popular my show was. There was nobody in town that didn't recognize me when I walked down the street, which is unbelievable for a public access show. But there were only thirty-five channels if you think about it and half of them didn't even go twenty-four hours. I was on at three in the morning on Saturday nights. It all makes sense.

Now there's five hundred channels, people have satellite dishes, and public access channels get totally lost in the shuffle. Times have changed. It's just not as popular. There's nobody anymore that goes, 'Did you see that public access show?' Unless they have a friend on it.

If you can get on TV in New York or LA, it's brilliant! It is so not a waste of time. But anywhere else, if you can get on a regular local affiliate or something like that, there's no way that's a waste of time either. Because you never know who's going to be watching. You just don't know.

How can anything you're putting out there be a waste of time? It's like going out to the clubs—you just never know. Even if there's only two people in the audience. What if there's just another comic you meet that's going to somehow change your life? It's all about getting out there. Because if you're doing local television, and even public access, you might meet somebody. You might even meet one of the camera guys that works on the show and he might be like, 'You know, my friend does this comedy show . . .' He might bring in this whole other thing. You just don't know.

One thing also can lead to another. I also had a show on the Food Network. It all led to everything because I was getting good notoriety from the public access show. I'd get more stage time at the clubs, because a lot of the owners saw it. They either loved it or hated it, but either way they saw it. That led to more stage time, which led to more people seeing me. The club owners already knew my bits, so it helped me with stand-up. They already knew my persona, which is the thing that helped get me on stage.

Anywhere you can get on the air is good. Any local television is excellent. You have to differ between local television and public access, but I think if you can get on any affiliated station with commercials and advertising to do a stand-up spot, that's great!

And yes, I did make Dave Attell a star. I have that film saved—it's my retirement fund. All those old tapes of Attell with hair!

FAQ 46 **What about Putting "Extras" on My Promo Tape?**

I did a show today for a charity and it actually went pretty well! Supposedly, I'm going to be interviewed on the local television newscast tonight. Is this something I should include on my promotional videotape? —T.K.

In this case—the news is good news! If the interview was aired, I hope you set your video recorder to tape the segment. If you didn't, find someone who can explain a VCR owner's manual for you and be better prepared next time. Another option is to call the station and find how you can get a copy. You'll probably be charged for this service, but consider it a cost toward promoting yourself.

Now, how you use this can depend on what you're looking for. If you're sending a tape to a talent booker to specifically work comedy clubs, he's not going to be too thrilled about watching a local newscast. He's only interested in your act and whether it would fit into his club. Chances are he'll hit the fast forward button until you are standing on stage in front of a live audience.

However, I'm from the school that says more is better than less when promoting yourself. A good television segment can add to your credibility and show you have some notoriety, at least in your area, or even nationally.

Its placement on your video is key in showing this. If you're sending it to someone only for bookings, put it at the end of your tape. They might not watch the segment, but even a brief glimpse could put the idea in their mind that you actually do have enough professional experience to be featured on television.

When you're looking for an agent or manager, the segment could serve as an introduction at the beginning, break up short comedy sets filmed at different clubs, or at the end for the same above reason. Be sure it presents you in a positive way and doesn't interrupt the flow of the comedy set you're using to get bookings. Even if the newscast only has a few seconds of your performance or an interview, it will show you were singled out for attention and are able to play for different events and audiences (in your case, a newsworthy charity).

It can also be argued that this technique can have an affect on someone "not in the business." This could include a corporate meeting planner or member of a college student activities board who doesn't meet someone everyday who's been on television. (Bookers, agents, and mangers do—so they're not as easily impressed). It might give you an element of "fame" and influence their decision in choosing an entertainer.

A few comics I've worked with have made guest appearances on popular television shows such as *Everybody Loves Raymond* or *The Drew Carey Show*. Sometimes they open the video with their appearance, or insert it at the end to add variety and credibility. Either way, it proves you're working and expanding yourself into different markets. Where it fits on the video depends on who's going to watch it.

Pat Wilson (Owner, Comedy West Agency, and Odyssey Management)

If they're sending me a videotape for management—yes, I want that included. If they're sending a video just for work, then all I want to see is their stand-up material. Because that's all I'm interested in. All that other stuff is just a lot of clutter.

This came up at a workshop I recently did in Boston. Everybody on the panel agreed that we don't want to see you being introduced by Jay Leno. We know by the backdrop that it's The Tonight Show. *We don't want it stretched out because we don't have a lot of time to look at videos. Also, you shouldn't edit your tape. As a booker, what I'm thinking is, "What did they edit out that they didn't want me to see?" We just want to see your material.*

That also goes for the promo package. All of us agreed on that panel, too. We want to see your résumé, your picture, and your tape. We don't want to see any newspaper articles. We don't want to see any of that other stuff. If we need it, we will ask you for it when we book you. That is, as a booker.

As a manager, if you're somebody I'm talking to about management, then, yes, I'm going to want that other stuff. When I want to manage a comedian, it's not necessarily just because they're funny. If I'm talking to you about management, I know you're funny. What I want to know is, can you act? Do you have an idea for a script or a treatment? Do you have a one-man show idea or are you doing a one-man show? Are you doing what it takes to get noticed in LA, besides just your stand-up comedy? So all that extra stuff gives me that.

FAQ 47 Am I a Comic, an Actor, or a Comic Actor?

I see a lot of stand-up comics acting in sitcoms, movies, and even commercials—both as stars and in supporting roles. I do a lot of different characters in my comedy sets and would love to get into acting. What's the best way to do this? —S.S.

Comedy and the acting profession have been walking together hand-in-hand since long before Bob Hope caught his first big screen look at Phyllis Diller in a fright wig. Comic stars from vaudeville, such as Charlie Chaplin, The Marx Brothers, and Hope himself, were cast in films to "act" the characters they had already developed through years of live performances. This proved to be a successful business concept for both the performers and the Hollywood film industry.

Many comedians point to the mid-eighties as the beginning of primetime for stand-ups on television. From Bill Cosby and Roseanne to Jerry Seinfeld, Tim Allen, Brett Butler, and Drew Carey—it seemed as if anyone who could get big laughs from a comedy club audience had a chance to star in their own network sitcom. But that trend was actually nothing new. Robin Williams is remembered as Mork from the seventies; and The Smothers Brothers starred in a sitcom, *The Smothers Brothers Show*, almost two years before their *Comedy Hour* variety series sent television censors diving for cover during the late sixties.

The keys to breaking into the acting business appear to be characters and personality, as well as an ability to make an audience laugh. If you're interested in making them cry, chances are you won't be discovered on a comedy stage and you should try your luck auditioning for soap operas.

Comedians have the opportunity to develop their characters and personalities on stage. If a casting director happens to see a performance and the comic fits a role or is interesting enough to develop a part based on his stage persona, then he could suddenly find himself writing "actor" on future tax returns. Steve Martin could act the jerk before he appeared on screen as *The Jerk*. Jim Carrey was a master of crazy characters before they were showcased on *In Living Color*. Tim Allen was talking about power tools pre-*Home Improvement*; Michael Richards was slipping on stage before he ever opened a door on *Seinfeld* as Kramer; and Roseanne was the disgruntled homemaker before given a household to run on her self-titled sitcom. These were already powerful characters before they were "discovered" and taken from the comedy club circuit into living rooms around the world.

Except acting is not an easy profession. The competition is tough, with numerous experienced and novice performers auditioning for the same role in what could potentially be a star-making production. With comedy clubs, there can be an underlining feeling of support that another comic does well so that the club stays open long enough for you to also get a booking. In acting? You either get the job or you don't.

There are similar business methods involved, such as having a head shot and résumé, but finding success as an actor demands more than an ability to hit your spot and making sure your best profile is toward the camera. Many comedians also attend classes and study acting techniques to help make their performances more real and alive for viewers—even if they play characters that are a bit crazy and over the top.

Suggestions for breaking into the acting biz can go hand-in-hand with your goal of becoming a good comedian. Dedicate yourself to being unique on stage and study your craft. Fully develop your character—your on-stage persona—and then find opportunities to be seen by casting directors, who are the bookers of the acting world. This might include partnership with an agent or manager with industry contacts, countless auditions, or the good fortune of appearing on stage at a showcase club or festival in front of producers looking to discover "the next big thing."

Ted Bardy (acting coach)

If they want to do commercials, which is a great field for comedians, they can often get hired from being seen in a comedy club. If they're doing different characters in their act, there's a certain personal style to each character. A lot of personality can be projected in the character work they do and in between the characters, as they go into each one.

Personality is big-time with commercials. A lot of that comes from being relaxed. Comedians can open up in front of audiences and know it's important to feel loose and relaxed. They work off the audience. But the biggest problem for a ot of comics is that when they get in front of the camera they don't have a club audience to work-off of. They start stiffening up and their personality doesn't come across—which is one of the big reasons why they were called into the audition to begin with.

If they're getting the opportunity to work in film or television, they have to know the style of the piece they're working in. If they're doing sitcoms, that's broad. They can go a bit over the top. But when they're working on a more naturalistic style film, they've got to play it a little closer to the vest. That's where training comes into play, and they might want to study some acting technique. At least a year's worth of study can get them really strong in that naturalistic style of acting.

I teach the Meisner Technique because it trains actors to work off of what's happening in front of them. It trains them to be truthful and honest. If they are working in an intimate medium like film and the style of the piece is naturalistic, they have to know that. They have to be truthful and honest in their actions and in what they're doing.

If they're working on the theatrical stage, they'll have to be "bigger"— though I ike to use the term "fuller"—so the audience in the back row knows what's going on. With a sitcom, they can also go "bigger" in the sense that the actions are "fuller."

There are plenty of comics who just can't act. As soon as they enter the room, the casting directors know they're not actors. The thing they need to know is that for commercials, they've got to convey their personality. For work in film and television, they've got to come across a bit as if they were a crafted actor—whether they've studied or not. They should have some coaching in the field to really sell themselves for television and film.

A great example of a comedian who's made the crossover into acting is Michael Keaton. He knows the style of the piece he's working in. He can do Beetlejuice, which is broad comedy and he's playing that strong character. But he can also do Clean and Sober, a great film and great work by Michael Keaton. It's truthful and honest—and he knew what the style of the piece was and what medium he was working in.

FAQ 48 How Do I Get to Letterman or Leno?

I guess I'm no different than a lot of comics out there. I want to be on Letterman or The Tonight Show. *Would I have to move to New York or Los Angeles? Do they look at videotapes? What's the best way to get booked on those shows? —C.H.*

It's very easy to say something sarcastic like the old joke, "How do you get to Carnegie Hall? Practice, practice, practice." How do you get on national television as a comedian? Be funny, funny, funny.

Honestly, that is the first step. You must be an experienced comic with a great set to get booked on the *Late Show with David Letterman* or *The Tonight Show with Jay Leno.* The comic may be making his national television debut, but rest assured it's not his first time on stage doing comedy.

When you honestly feel you're as good or better than some of the comedians you see on these programs, then it's time to make the effort to be seen by the show's talent coordinator. Yes, they will watch videotapes. But I believe you have a better chance performing regularly at clubs they use for showcasing or being recommended by another comic or someone within the industry that the talent booker respects.

From my experience as the talent coordinator for A&E's *An Evening At The Improv*, the best way to be seen is to be part of the scene. In other words, on stage at the better clubs and comedy festivals where your talent can be regularly showcased.

When I worked in New York City and Los Angeles, I was able to see a lot of comedians on a regular basis. It was quite obvious to myself and the other television bookers, agents, and managers who frequented the club, which acts were ready for our respective projects. All we had to do was walk up and ask them to do our shows.

We also watched countless videotapes from comics who were not in our area. But I personally only ever booked one for the television show based solely on his tape. That was a comedian named Tommy Blaze who simply had me laughing throughout—and there was no doubt in my mind he could do the show. There were many others who were also very funny, but I waited until they were in Los Angeles and scheduled them for three-minute showcases at The Improv. Some made the cut and were booked for the show, while others were unfortunately not ready for national television.

The most reliable method to get booked for national television is to have the talent coordinator see you perform on a regular basis. When a comic continually has great sets, booking them is almost a no-brainer.

So . . . do you have to move to New York or Los Angeles to be seen for one of these shows? Not necessarily. As I mentioned, a videotape could get you an audition the next time you're there. But in some cases . . . well, if you want to be a movie star, you go to Hollywood. If you want to be on *Letterman* or *The Tonight Show*, you go where the talent coordinators can see you.

But (and that's an important *but*), lightening can strike almost anywhere. A chance booking with another act who can give you that valuable referral, performing at a comedy festival, or winning a prestigious contest can get you noticed by the right people. The idea is to be prepared, ambitious, and of course, funny, funny, funny. . . .

Eddie Brill

I really work hard at it. I really take it seriously. And the one thing I have to keep in mind—and always the comedians who approach me have to keep in mind—is that it's not The Eddie Brill Show. It's The Letterman Show. I know what kind of comics he would like and would fit the style of the show.

I go to comedy festivals. I get videotapes and I look at them. I also set up showcases in New York and LA. But pretty much I know most of the comedians. The people I don't know, I have friends all over and I ask them to look out for comedians for me—if it's from someone I respect. Because it's like advertising— 'Hey, I have this great client and they're on this TV show and they've opened for this person . . . ' And I'm saying, do they have four-and-a-half-minutes that are smart and clever and [are they a] monologist? In a monologist form? And if they have that, they could be a grocery bagger as long as they have that set that I need. I worked [as a comic] in the Midwest with someone I thought was funny and it worked out. I worked with this one kid at Caroline's one Monday night on New Talent Night and he ended up doing the show.

People are, you know, begging agents and, 'Can I have my guy open for Eddie on the road?' But I don't let it drive me nuts. That's the whole thing. First of all, I'm a comedian. I understand what other comedians are doing. I don't blame them. They'd be idiots for not wanting me to see them. I think that's why being a stand-up comic makes a big difference. And I've really learned how to craft the set. You know, the art of the four-and-a-half-minute set. I've learned how to edit very well and I can help them with their editing. As a comedian, you can't see what other people can. I don't have to do it that many times. If the material is already there, it's just a matter of rhythms and editing. Sometimes I can see what they can't see.

FAQ 49 Got Any Tips for Breaking into the College Market?

I want to get into the college market. I get really great response in clubs from a younger crowd, like students. I guess it's because we're close to the same age and I have material they can relate to. How would I do this? —B.D.

How would you do this? My suggestion is to book shows at colleges. Uh . . . wait a minute. That answer would definitely earn me a solid F if this were an exam. To raise the grading curve, here's an overview of College Marketing 101. The 201 course, of course, will follow. . . .

College shows (which for our purposes also includes universities, junior colleges, and trade schools) can have a very different audience than what you'd normally encounter in a comedy club. For one thing, they're younger. Clubs with liquor licenses have age restrictions and most college students cannot enter legally without their parents or adult supervision. These venues can turn off the beer kegs and host special events, such as prom shows or youth groups, but for the most part they cater to audiences over the age of twenty-one. If you understand the economics behind nightclubs, you'll know that liquor sales can often pay the rent.

The majority of college students also enjoy a different style of comedy than an older generation. This is evident by the "teen movies" produced in Hollywood. The plots often involve first dates, first sex, first drink, first year in college, and other subjects they can relate to firsthand. This is common with all age groups and is why some films are specifically aimed at different demographics, from pre-schoolers to senior citizens. As always in the entertainment business, it's knowing your audience.

We'll talk more about this in the next section, but here's a hint: be prepared to work clean. You should also have an hour's worth of material, even though you can still be building up to that time frame during your college market orientation.

If you're confident your material is suited for student audiences, it's time to start building your college résumé credits. For reasons once again explained in our following 201 course, a seasoned comedian should consider working with a college booking agent. When compared to the club circuit, this is a very different system to work in. Student activities departments and college agencies can be a tight-knit group and it could take a large financial investment, pages of application forms, stacks of promotional material, and countless phone calls just to get an opportunity to be seen by someone who has the authority to book shows on a college campus. College agents do this for a living and are already familiar with the territory.

But if you're not yet ready for a college agent, don't drop out. Even a beginning comedian can start laying the groundwork for getting on-campus experience and résumé credits, which should eventually attract a college agent. Here's a way to do just that. . . .

Student activities departments have budgets for performers and events. They try to spend their money wisely, so an unknown without the backing of a reliable college agent will probably not headline a gala Parent's Weekend show in the school auditorium. However, students can still be entertained at other on-campus areas. Afternoon shows (nooners, as comics call them) in cafeterias or student unions are very popular. There are also various clubs and organizations, such as theater departments, fraternities, and sororities, that could be interested in a comedy show for a special meeting or event.

Many of these groups—and even student activities departments—can be approached in almost the same way as a potential open-mike room. In other words, they should be interested in free entertainment.

A good idea is to research colleges near you, find out how to contact these various groups, and suggest a free comedy show. Promise clean material (you'll most likely have to provide a video to prove it) and agree on a certain length of time for the performance. If you know other comics interested in breaking into the market, ask them to join you in these shows and each do shorter sets while working on college-style material. This will not only give you valuable experience in front of a student audience, but also a list of résumé credits that could impress a college agent, who can then use them to impress a college booker.

Of course you can still book paying shows without a college agent through the contacts suggested above. But to really be successful, there's a lot more work involved than making a phone call, traveling to a school and going on stage. With that lesson in the books, it's time to graduate into College Marketing 201. . . .

Kate Magill (College Agent, Owner of Sophie K. Entertainment)

Get a clean, clear videotape and have an hour of material. And by clear, I mean I want to see the comedian's face. You'd be surprised at some of the tapes I get where you can't even tell what they look like! And I would tell the comedian not to worry so much about showing the audience. Just worry about your material. Because if they like your material and it's strong enough, the students will like you.

I hesitate to book comedians that have material about being older in age. Mainly because it's a harder sell. Because students have never been divorced, they've never been married, or had children. Most of them anyway, you know. It's something they haven't come across yet in life. So therefore, they don't find it as funny.

As far as using the F-word, it depends. I would talk to the director and ask their opinion first. And don't believe what the students tell you is okay. Because they will always tell you that you can say it.

The cleaner you keep it, the more places you can work. You can do everything if you're clean. You can do orientations, family weekends . . . You'll never be out of work if you can write clean—and you're funny.

FAQ 50 **Okay, You Promised Us College Marketing 201. So, What Are NACA and APCA?**

I've been hearing a lot about NACA and APCA from other comics who are working colleges. I know they have these big conventions with students and college agents where they do showcases and get bookings. What's up with that? —L.B.

There's something to be said for the motto: "Give it that old college spirit!" Whether it was the rally cry to win a football game or take over a town as in *Animal House*, it's a rah-rah, high-energy way to get something done. The same idea can be true when working in the college entertainment market.

In general, colleges have one thing in common. They're well organized. This starts with the requirements for administration and staff, and goes right through to the student body with class schedules, dorm assignments, and campus activities. You'll also find a lot of rah-rah spirit and enough high-energy to power everything from all-night study groups to weekend-long parties.

This also is the way most colleges book entertainment. Yes, a performer without a college agent can still schedule shows, but a better way is to be organized. And the organizations involved in this business specialize in high-energy, rah-rah spirited events when it comes to campus programming (which is the scholastic term for booking shows).

Comedians, as well as any performer, lecturer, or promoter looking to work in the college market (within the United States), should be aware of two organizations formed specifically for this purpose: National Association for Campus Activities (NACA) and Association for the Promotion of Campus Activities (APCA). Each charges a yearly membership fee based on different categories (buyer or seller) and how many regions of the country in which you plan to work. Members include schools, agencies, and performers who follow specific requirements and business methods to accomplish their shared goal of bringing events to campuses.

Both NACA and APCA are based on the technique of "cooperative (co-op) buying," or as it's also called, "block-booking." The idea allows schools to save money on entertainment costs, while offering performers more work, and therefore, more money in the long run.

For example, let's say a comedian charges $1,000 for a single college performance. If three schools in the same region agree to book him for shows within a five-day period, they would form a co-op to get a lesser price. In that case, the comic's price might be $850 per show, saving each school $150 while he earns $2,550. If five schools book him within seven days, his co-op price could be $800 per show, saving each school $200 and earning himself $4,000 for the week.

Now, you might think if the comedian stuck to his original price, he would walk away with an extra $1,000. But that's not how the organized college market works. Like most businesses, student activities boards have budgets and are looking to get the most for their money. Co-op buying allows them to cut costs and even use the extra savings to bring more entertainment to their schools. The comedian may still book shows at his top price, but chances are he'll get more work and earn more money with this method.

The main difference between NACA and APCA is size. The former has almost 1,100 member colleges, while the latter works with about 200.

Each has an advantage over the other when it comes to promoting yourself in front of college buyers, which will be explained after this explanation. . . .

As a performer, the goal is to showcase for these schools, which is done at annual programming conferences held by both organizations in different regions. NACA divides the country into seven regions: South, Mid-America, Mid-Atlantic, Central, Northeast, West, and Northern Plains. APCA has two: Northeast and Houston. Both organizations host a programming conference in each region, along with a larger national conference each year that all member schools may attend. Representatives from student programming boards looking to book entertainment attend the conference in their school's and/or the national regions.

Colleges may book performers based on the recommendation of an agent (usually one they've worked with in the past), or through contacts with local clubs, recommendations from students, or other "being in the right place at the right time" methods. But nothing can beat a live showcase in front of an auditorium full of student buyers.

The advantage APCA offers is a guaranteed conference showcase for agency or performer members. The NACA advantage is the chance to put your act in front of more schools, but a showcase is not guaranteed. Many agencies belong to both organizations, while individual performers might rely on economics to decide their loyalty. The total investment to attend a three-day programming conference can be expensive (membership, exhibit-hall booth fees, promotional material, travel, hotel, meals, etc.), so a performer might choose to break in with APCA for the guaranteed showcase. At least the money spent will get him on stage, but as is true with both organizations, there are no guarantees of bookings.

Gaining a showcase at an NACA conference involves paperwork, deadlines, and an excellent videotape. Basically, it's a lot of work, but a successful showcase makes it worth the effort.

Most NACA conferences are held in the fall of the year; the national and one of the regionals are in late winter. Applications to showcase need to be submitted months in advance to each conference you plan to attend. These are reviewed by a board made up of students from different schools within the region who make the decisions on who will be awarded showcases.

The showcase applications for all regions are sent out to members in the spring. The forms to be filled out and returned include pages for contact information, prices for a singular performance, and block-bookings, the performer's bio (no longer than 150 words), and detailed on-stage technical requirements. Even if you require only a microphone and a stand, a diagram showing where these items are to be placed on stage must be drawn and labeled on this last form. (And if you want a stool to place a glass of water on, you must show that, also!)

Eight copies of each form are needed for every region you apply to, along with copies of your head shot. Include the required showcase application fee and cost for a promotional booth at the conference, a video of your set (only one copy is needed for each region), and send before the application deadline. In approximately two months you'll receive a letter from each board with their decision about your showcase.

If you get a positive answer, you'll have a twenty-minute showcase (exactly— there will be a clock facing you on stage counting down the minutes and seconds) and a promotional booth during the three-day conference. You will also be charged an additional showcase fee to help pay for stage lighting, sound equipment, and the stage hands needed to set it up and tear it down. If the reply is negative, you still own a booth in the exhibit hall to promote yourself to students, but not a showcase opportunity.

To put this into perspective, I was told at an NACA Regional Conference that over four hundred showcase submissions were received for forty available spots. This not only included comedians, but also bands, lecturers, variety acts, and everyone else looking to book college shows. To say the least, competition is intense.

This is why having a college agent makes a lot of sense. They pay the membership and booth fees (and we're talking thousands of dollars if they attend most regionals and the national) while their represented acts are charged the showcase submission fee (in the $35 to $40 area) and performance fee (approximately $200). The agents work at the conference for the entire three days (paying for accommodations and meals) while the performer needs only to be present on the day he showcases (fly in, fly out, and go hungry, if you prefer).

There are also other considerations when applying for a showcase. The type of act and co-op price can determine what category you are submitting for. Every showcase needs an MC, which makes it a great position for a comedian because he can get on stage quickly, do a five-minute set while the stage crew works behind him to prepare for the next act, and then introduce that performer. If there are five acts on the showcase, the MC will have five opportunities in front of the crowd for a total of twenty-five minutes—which is five more than the other performers.

The coffee house category is usually for acts who can perform on a smaller stage and are more economically priced. The main stage showcase is where you'll find bigger bands, performance troupes, or comedians with solid credits, some name recognition in the college market, and a higher price. Except none of this is written in stone and displayed in a campus trophy case. The student committee will make the final decision on where you will showcase and in what position. If it doesn't fit the category you chose on your application, they'll contact you for permission. Of course you'll agree. . . .

In addition to all the forms, the committees will base their showcase decisions on your videotape. This will prove whether or not you're "right" for the college market and how you rate next to the competition.

Videos are required to be three minutes long. But here's a hint—don't stop there. A very knowledgeable and experienced comedian will explain this better in a moment, but be aware that three minutes can only get you past the first round of judging. It's a good idea to submit ten to twelve minutes of your best material, geared for a college audience. Remember, most students haven't personally experienced "adult" subjects such as marriage, divorce, or having children, so as a group they're not going to be too interested in that type of material.

One trap comedians fall into is writing what they "think" is a college-worthy set. Yes, good topics for students can be sex, drugs, beer, and skipping classes—but you shouldn't promote these vices as being the best options on earth. And under no circumstances at a college showcase should you use graphic sexual material or drop the infamous F-bomb four-letter word. Unless, of course, you want the microphone shut off during your showcase and no bookings for your conference investment. In colleges, "clean" is the word.

Once you think about the situation, it's easy to understand. Students attending the conferences are chaperoned by advisors from the school's programming board. In other words, organized adults who are essentially a censor board for what activities will take place at their wholesome campus. In addition to the students, administration, parents, alumni, benefactors, and other influential people may also attend these shows. The bottom line is not to offend anyone, and programming advisors are not about to risk their jobs by letting that happen. When you secure a booking and arrive at the campus to do your show, ask the advisor what restrictions they have—and follow them to the letter. Some students may cheer if you go off course into four-letter land, but chances are you won't be invited back when the same advisor attends next year's conference with a different group of wholesome students.

The actual exhibit hall at a programming conference can be compared to a large trade show filled with college rah-rah spirit. Similar to walking down aisles of car or boat dealerships, students "shop" for entertainment at booths set-up by agencies and performers. Each booth is individually decorated with banners, signs, posters of acts, performance video loops on giant televisions, and tables displaying promotional material. Sometimes flashing lights, music, and even bowls of candy or other giveaways are used to draw students' attention away from competitors and into a practiced sales pitch.

Many performers will follow their showcase with a personal appearance at their agent's booth to sign autographs, while impressed students fill out co-op buying forms declaring interest in bringing that act to their campus. These forms require the name of the college, dates they're interested in booking the act, and signature of the school's designated co-op buyer. Agencies include their information, signature, and an identification number. Both keep one copy, while a third is given to the co-op board, which also has a booth in the exhibit hall.

Conferences are all day-long, weekend events that can run until well after midnight with numerous showcases, exhibit halls, educational and training sessions, box lunches, sit-down meals with guest speakers, dances, mixers, and agency gab sessions at the hotel bar (where underage students are not allowed). But the most anticipated events are the co-op meetings normally held after each day's final showcase and exhibit hall.

These meetings, moderated by members of the co-op board, are where agents and performers work with interested schools to form block-bookings. A performer's name is announced and any school buyer who has filled-out a co-op form for that act will raise his hand. When three or more hands are in the air, a block-booking will be attempted. If the requirements are met for the performer's advertised co-op deal (say, three shows within five days), the discounted price is awarded and both parties agree to sign a contract. When forming numerous blocks in numerous regions, a college performer can book his entire year through these conferences.

This concludes your undergraduate course in College Marketing 201. Grad school begins once you attend your first college booking conference and learn more details about the business and promotional methods used by the top college agents and performers. For an online field trip, visit *www.naca.org* and *www.apca.com*.

Brad Lowery

To get into the college market, you have to actually go to a NACA Convention; the National Association for Campus Activities. For a showcase submission, one of the delegates told me that to get them to choose you, you should actually have four, three minute sets. What the selection committee does is watch the first three minutes. If they like you, they put you over on the left. If they don't, they put you on the right. Then after they go through all the other tapes, they come back and watch another round of you. Then they watch another three minutes to see if you go on to be in what they sort of call the finals. In other words, the final pick. And they don't rewind at all. They just pick up from where they left off. This way, if they like you in those first three sets of three minutes, there's a good chance the next one will get you in the showcase.

Just have your set divided. In other words, you would end a joke at three minutes. Then just start a whole, fresh new joke. You know what I mean? That's what it's about. That's what they look for.

A lot of comics showcase and just do their regular set. When you're performing in front of a large audience like that, it's more like being "in-concert." So in other words, you have to give all the energy you can for all these kids to really get into it.

I MC at a lot of the conventions. I'm high-energy, I play with the kids, and pretty much give them what they want. So for an upcoming comic, if they're on number two as far as their speed, they have to bring it up to number five. They have to exert their energy and get it out to where the kids are like, 'Wow! This guy is full of energy!'

Never let anything distract you during a showcase, because there's a lot going on behind you. They can't close the curtains on stage, so if they're working behind you setting up for the next act, don't pay any attention to that. Believe it or not, I got a crazy amount of work out of being like that. I never let them distract me.

With NACA showcases, there are some comedians who will actually take a chance when it comes to working clean. They'll say, 'Well, if I get the work—I'll get it.' And some say, 'If I don't, I don't.' But, at the convention you have to be clean or a lot of the colleges will just shy away from you. I've always been clean, so I've never had a problem. After you get booked at a college, the best way to do it is to ask the people who are in charge. What can I do and what can't I do? That's the best way to get around it.

I had a college . . . Sacred Heart College in Connecticut. They had called the agency for a Def Comedy Jam comic and they sent me. And even though I did Def Comedy Jam, I was one of the first comics to do it clean. So when they asked for a Def Comedy Jam comic, I asked why are you sending me?

When I got there, the lady said, "You can't talk about sex, you can't talk about drinking, you can't talk about drugs . . ." There were so many restrictions. I told her, "Look, let me do my set. If you don't like it, you don't have to pay me." And I got paid. But I watched her as she cringed every time I brought up one of the subjects she told me not to. Then after she saw it, she was relieved. I could see her, as they say, waiting to exhale.

Another thing the colleges like is when you stick around for a few minutes, for like a "meet and greet." A lot of them really like that. And if you shy away from it, they'll actually put that in the programming guide to let other colleges know that you're not personable. They just want to talk with you for a few minutes, just to say hello or whatever. You don't have to just rush right off. The same people that you see on the way up are the same people you're gonna see on the way down.

Also, pay your taxes! Especially if you're going to do the college market. I've actually had comedians call me from Chicago and down south, because they had gotten a large number of colleges and their agents told them to call me. I told them the thing they need to know the most is to be sure to pay your taxes. Otherwise, they're gonna come after you! A lot of comics just ignore it and they end up in a lot of trouble.

FAQ 51 What's the Deal with Corporate Shows?

I've been told by other comics that I don't have the right act or the right look for corporate shows, but also that it pays a lot more than doing clubs. I'd be willing to change for that reason alone! How would I do this? —M.P.

How would you change? I'd guess a healthy diet, self-help books, or the Witness Protection Program could do the trick. Then again, if it's strictly comedy you're referring to, then you'd need to change into a "corporate comedian."

In these times of morale-boosting, highly technical training, and efforts at stress reduction in the business world, corporations and private companies schedule various events for their employees. These can include holiday parties, award banquets, in-house training, golf outings, and any number of reasons to get them more inspired, productive, and happy. An important aspect is also to build a feeling of "family" and as a team working to achieve a common positive goal.

Since the main reason to hold these gatherings is the business itself, you can buy stock in the fact the CEO will speak about the state of company affairs and invest a few moments telling inside jokes about key employees. But "family" gatherings are supposed to be festive (no offense to all you CEOs), and a smart meeting planner knows a good way to do this is by hiring a professional entertainer.

The corporate market can be a lucrative one for comedians willing to play by the rules. What are the rules? Having the right act and the right look is a good start, but this is also where knowing your audience helps. After all, it's "corporate."

Think about who will be attending this event. Business people are no strangers to regular work hours, office etiquette, and business attire. In other words, it's the "straight world," which is the polar opposite of a club's midnight show with a comic in torn jeans holding a microphone in one hand and a beer in the other.

I'll say it again. It's "corporate."

This is not to say some members of the corporate audience wouldn't rather be in a club and drinking beer during the late show. But it could be uncomfortable sitting next to the boss and his wife, the uptight paper shuffler who occupies the adjoining cubicle, and a new office hotshot looking to advance his career at any expense. Especially when the employee-in-question laughs at the exact moment his boss' wife takes offense to a joke.

Corporate comedy is safe and doesn't offend anyone in the room. There is no swearing or graphic sexual material. Slight innuendoes can be acceptable, along with mentions of alcohol and drug use as being funny—but only if the end result explains why it's called "dope" in the first place. Business and personal relationships, in-office humor, the company "family" and products, competitors, finances, current events, and general observations are safe topics. When it comes to a comic's performance, a PG-13 rating would be considered living on the edge.

For comedians who work clean, performing at a corporate show can be as easy as wearing a suit and doing their regular act. For others it means writing new material that won't necessarily go over at midnight shows, but will earn big laughs at a corporate function.

Once you understand "the rules" and have made a decision to work in this market, you'll probably have to make adjustments to your act. Corporate shows can usually range from fifteen minutes to an hour. Gear some references in your material toward the business world, such as changing one of your characters into a supervisor, or an antagonist into the company's competitor, and do your best to make sure a crowd of various ages can relate to any personal experiences or observations you choose to talk about.

Even without an agent or recognizable name, you can still break into the corporate market. Search the library for reference books on organizations, charities, and member clubs, then volunteer your services—for free—as entertainment. Doing this will give you experience and a "feel" for this type of audience. If you do well, ask for a letter of recommendation. If not, rewrite your act and try again.

After you have experience and credits on your résumé, search for businesses that have events and begin the process of marketing yourself for paid engagements. This can be done similar to the way you contact bookers, by finding the name of the person in charge of events and sending your material. Do a follow-up phone call and stay in touch with an occasional postcard.

For a professional look when it comes to promotional material, many corporate comics use a two-, three-, or four-fold brochure. This is more convenient for meeting planners than keeping a full promotional package on file. It's also a good idea to mail brochures instead of postcards because of the amount of information (advertising) it holds.

A brochure should include the highlights of your promo package in an abbreviated form. A small headshot with contact information can go on the cover, along with a few lines from a supportive letter of recommendation. Inside can be credits, bio information, photos, and more rave reviews. A professional typesetter can help design an eye-catching brochure and could be worth the investment.

As hinted at above, it's always a good idea to personalize your performance toward the audience. If done correctly, it can help impress meeting planners and audience members into recommending you for other events. Here's a great idea on how to do this:

Meeting planners like the security of a contract with performers. Since I'm not a lawyer, I'll steer you once again to a library where there are many resources containing sample contracts. You basically need your name, the company, and contact person's name, date, time, location, and length of show, your fee and any special provisions such as travel, accommodations, meal, and a microphone with a stand. These are all discussed and agreed upon when booking the engagement. Monetary deposits are also used to hold the date and a 50 percent return with a signed contract is not unusual. The remainder can be paid before or at the show.

Now, here's the idea. Along with the contract, send a questionnaire to be filled out about the event and returned with the deposit. This will give you specific information to personalize the show. The one I use includes space to name the president, supervisors, and any key employees. Also company products, make-up of the audience (employees, clients, spouses, etc.), planned attendance, competitor's names, local hangouts, and any anecdotes they'd like to share about the company.

Language and sexual content are two concerns that meeting planners will lose sleep over before an engagement. Show you're aware of this by coming right out and asking about it on the questionnaire. Have a scale from one to ten for each. Over the number one, write "clean as newly fallen snow," while ten could be "anything goes" (you're funnier than I am, so use your creativity for these headings). The meeting planner can circle a preference at either end or anywhere in between. Of course, a good corporate comic will still remember PG-13 is living on the edge, but the meeting planner will be better rested.

Whether it's corporate comedy or a midnight show, the goal is always laughter. You may need to invest in better clothes and a haircut, but after all— it's corporate.

Richard Jeni

I didn't know about [corporate gigs], but then people started calling me after, you know, after you get exposure on television. People started calling and then it became a big part of my business.

I like them in the sense that they pay really good and you don't have to get up at six o'clock in the morning and go on the wacky morning radio show to promote your gig for Xerox. But ultimately it's not as much fun as doing your show in a club or a theater or where people are coming to see "you." The corporate gig, it's like their party and you happen to be there.

You basically do the same act without the curse words. You gotta clean it up and you gotta be . . . You know, it's corporate! And I have nooooo problem with that. Gimme the money—I'm your bitch!

Everybody does corporate gigs, really. Everybody from Bill Cosby to Jay Leno on down. And it's a part of the business that nobody talks about very much.

FAQ 52 What's the Going Rate?

I'd like your take on going rates for corporate and private parties. I guess it's what the market will bear, but I'd like your expert opinion. —D.H.

My "expert opinion" comes from years of being in the market. The supermarket, that is. I'm the guy who stands in the longest checkout lines just to read the tabloids without paying for them. My opinion? Most stars shouldn't leave home without wearing make-up, multiple marriages make for multiple headlines—and rich people like to throw parties.

The same can be said about corporate events. Smaller companies on a shoestring budget are going to lay low until their financial makeup allows them to spend more on festive activities. The larger ones with multiple incomes are going to throw parties to keep their employees happy; while also letting the public know they're successful, "So buy from me!" Then again, a lot of that money can go into the advertising budget or paying for multiple marriages by the boss. But even when they scrape up the loose cash, some of these companies can throw one heck of a bash.

So let's look at the entertainment budget for an average corporate event. There's the cost of renting a ballroom, meeting hall, or conference room. Dinner will probably be served, along with a cocktail hour on the company's tab and a staff of caterers and servers to dish out and pour everything. Table decorations, gifts, and favors might be waiting for employees and guests at their seats, or the company may even pay for travel and accommodations for an out-of-town event.

This may seem extravagant (and for some companies it is), but it's also not uncommon. Cities and resorts are always looking to book large conventions, and corporations are among their biggest clients. There's a lot of money changing hands, which translates into earning possibilities for corporate entertainers.

What's the going rate? You're correct in saying the market will determine your price. Some companies have a specific budget they won't go over, regardless of what type of entertainment they're shopping for. Others have a specific performer in mind, will find out his price, and have a "corporate meeting" to decide if they're willing to pay it.

Much depends on the act's credits. A comedian who's been on *The Tonight Show* will command more than an open-mike regular. Even a meeting planner who is new in the business will grasp the economics of that proposition.

By the time you have national television appearances on your résumé, it's safe to say you'll have an agent who understands how to negotiate in the corporate market. But just to give you an idea, plan to make as much or more than you would for an entire week's booking at one club. Chances are a corporate show will fall on one of those evenings, so you wouldn't be able to fulfill your club booking that week. Since clubs expect you to appear when scheduled, you'd need to decide if one corporate event can make-up for the earnings you'd lose by giving up multiple shows and leaving that week open.

The best scenario is booking an afternoon corporate appearance in the same city you're appearing in that night. Meeting planners often call clubs to recommend a comedian. When it happens to be the same date you're in town, the club booker can ask how much you'd charge to give up an afternoon of watching television in your hotel room and take a percentage by scheduling the extra show. There's also no reason why you can't work in advance by researching companies and organizations in the area you'll be traveling to, and then mail brochures.

When you're starting out in the corporate market, you'll probably be glad to accept whatever is offered. Again, this will add to your experience and résumé. If it means taking time away from your day job or personal life, set a price to make it worth your while. But you must be honest with yourself—can you do an hour of clean and funny corporate-style material? If the answer is yes, then start playing the economy.

Assuming you're an "unknown," it's wise to start low as you're building a career. But before we get too far below the pay chart, here are a few things to consider:

1. Meeting planners will sometimes ask if they can pay less for a shorter show. You can use this if it works for you in negotiating, but most performers feel if they're leaving home—regardless of whether it's five minutes or two hours—they should still be paid the same fee. After all, you can't make any other plans for that afternoon or evening because you've been hired to work.

2. You might take less pay on an off night, which would usually be a Sunday, Monday, or Tuesday. You still can schedule that weekend in a club and earn extra money on a day you normally aren't scheduled to work.

3. Be sure you charge enough to cover costs for travel and accommodations, unless it's a simple drive and you're sleeping in your own bed that same night. It's not uncommon to ask that a hotel room be provided on top of your fee or include what it would cost to stay overnight.

Ask what the company budget is for a comedian. Some meeting planners will come right out and tell you, while others want to know what you charge. Ask how many people will be attending the event. This may not even influence what you'll charge for the booking, but it lets them know they're negotiating with a professional.

You could use a per-person price. For instance, a person going to a comedy club might pay $10 to see the show. In the corporate world, you could keep the same price, or negotiate at a different figure for a "special event." If you decide $5 a person is fair and there are 100 people at the event, you would charge $500.

If you're still up in the air without a net, it's time to set your price. For our purposes, let's say $200. If the meeting planner agrees, you accept the job. If not, ask for a counter-offer and make your decision. This is negotiating.

If $200 is your price, keep it while you work at scheduling other shows. When you learn firsthand the market is willing to pay more for what you're offering, gradually increase your fee. By the time you get on national television, corporate show earnings could help pay for multiple marriages—or at least enough makeup so you look better on the front page of the supermarket tabloids.

Bobby Collins

I love a corporate gig. It challenges me as a comedian, rather than working in a the-ater or a club where people come to see you; like in Las Vegas or a resort area. Most of these people really don't know who you are, so it kind of keeps you humble.

It's always easier when you walk out and half, or three quarters or all of them came to see you. That's what they're paying for. Some don't know you, but their friends drag them along. But now in a corporate gig, they don't know you at all. Maybe the guy . . . the president and his secretary saw your tape, or they needed a comic to come in, or 'My wife likes this guy, Bobby Collins'—which is how I get a lot of gigs.

Then I go in there and to me, it's not only a humble experience, but it's an experience that challenges me. Because now I can convert another seven hundred people that have a lot of money and have influence to come out to see me when-ever I'm playing somewhere else. Also to get other corporate jobs, because word-of-mouth in corporations is huge. So it's always a win-win situation for me when I go on a corporate gig because I can further my audience and get other jobs. Those are the type of jobs you want because they pay a lot more than the jobs on the road.

Most of the time, corporations challenge you. And I love that challenge. That separates the men from the boys. I just love that because most comics I see don't know how to work a big stage.

FAQ 53 **Do You Think I Should Sell Stuff after My Show?**

A lot of times I'll see comics selling merchandise after their shows. CDs, cassettes, T-shirts, bumper stickers—you name it, they seem to sell it. Sometimes the last part of their show is just a commercial for this stuff. I'd like the extra money, but am not sure I want to end each night as a traveling salesman. —T.R.

Some people are born salesmen. They can talk their way into an audition, be persuasive when dealing with bookers, and sell merchandise to audiences after a show. For them, it's no problem and just another aspect of being in showbiz.

Sports teams and rock bands put their names and logos on various items for profit. Celebrities endorse products and make commercials and personal appearances to increase business. Then again, many are careful of what they sell and how it might affect their image. A quarterback might promote his likeness on a bobblehead doll, while a serious writer could refuse if he thought it would cheapen the message in his work.

How you look at merchandizing is a personal choice. We'd all enjoy an extra stream of income, but how comfortable would you feel hawking your wares from the stage, then making change for customers in the back of the room? For some it's no problem. For others, it cheapens their message.

Comedians sit on both sides of the fence in this debate. Some can make huge profits on merchandise and may even take less pay for a performance knowing the difference can be made up with after-show sales. Others feel it's not worth it to travel with the extra luggage, and feel more comfortable making their money on stage.

Your place in the show can also help in making a decision about selling merchandise. There's no rule saying an MC can't sell CDs of his performance, but it could be a lonely shift if the headliner everyone came to see is doing the same at the next table.

If you're committed to selling merchandise, choose an item that is a unique remembrance of your performance. A professionally recorded CD or cassette from an earlier show is always a good bet. If the audience loved you live, this is the next best thing to reliving that experience. If you have a trademark line or a hook, it could work on a T-shirt or bumper sticker. Some of your material or humorous essays could be illustrated and made into a self-published book. The ideas are endless, if you're creative and think like a salesman.

One final thought about merchandizing. Running a commercial for your products during the show can be annoying to an audience that has already paid admission and is only interested in laughing. It might help your image to make the announcement funny, or at least be brief and to the point—then make them laugh hard enough to buy at the end of the show.

Flip Orley

I have CDs and I don't make a big to-do about the fact that I have CDs. Initially, I didn't have anything like that, because I didn't want to market stuff. Have you ever gone to see a bar band and they're spending, like, half of their set trying to sell their CD? Comics are as bad, if not worse than that.

My whole attitude is if I like what you're doing, shut-up, do your set, and if I like your stuff, I'll buy your stuff at the end of the night. Don't make this like an infomercial. So consequently, since I feel that way when I'm in the audience, I certainly don't want to become that when I'm on stage. So I never mention my CDs, which isn't great for sales. But be that as it may, I don't mention my CDs in my show. At the end of the night, most times I do, but sometimes I even forget. I'll say, "Oh, by the way, if you're interested in using hypnosis for self-improvement, I've got some CDs. Feel free to check my Web site." And that's the extent of it.

I'm the first to admit I'm not the best at selling myself. I've never really been great at self-promotion. I wish I could be. But again, watching comics sell their CDs or their "eyeballs" or things of that nature off the stage, I find that uncomfortable in the audience, so I don't want to do that on stage. So people that are really big self-promoters, a lot of times I find obnoxious. So I don't do it well.

FAQ 54 **What If I Want to Publish My Comedy Material as a Book?**

I am very interested in how to go about doing a book proposal. A comedian I worked with made me promise to write a book about, as he put it, my "very interesting life." He also said I could sell copies after my shows.

Needless to say, I've written quite a bit (I know I didn't write this much in grad school!). I could really use your opinions and know-how to get this finished and published. —M.G.

I was going to write a book about my life, but every time I went through the torture of trying to get it published, the experience would demand another chapter. After writing it and looking again for a publisher, it was apparent I needed to write an additional chapter about that process. If this continues, I'll never be finished—and I doubt anyone would find my story very interesting.

When you're searching for your first book deal, it's important to have the entire manuscript finished—mainly because you won't have a track record to prove you are capable of authoring a book. Publishers and literary agents may be contacted through a brief proposal and sample chapters, but if someone expresses interest, you'll be ready with a completed project.

Publishers can be similar to casting directors, which means they sometimes will not accept "unsolicited submissions." In these cases, you will need representation. In the writing world, this person is defined as a literary agent who can make "solicited submissions" and take a percentage of the author's earnings.

There are numerous books available listing publishers and literary agents, along with contact information, type of projects they handle, and submission guidelines. You'll find that some of these "right people" could be the "wrong people" for you, because they only work with certain topics and avoid others.

One of these many resources is *Writer's Market*, which is updated every year. It has mainly information about publishers and magazines, but also includes a very good section on how to write query letters and make submissions. If you use the information from the *Writer's Market*, along with a resource listing literary agents, you should be able to develop a professional-looking submission package and figure out where to send it. You can also find information about self-publishing and getting into the e-book market (where your book is produced in a downloadable electronic format, which can be purchased and acquired online).

Since there are too many of these resource books for me to single out, I suggest you visit a larger bookstore, purchase a café latte, and start browsing. But remember to keep an eye on the date the book was published. Just like our agent friends in the performing world, literary agents can make career changes at a fast rate. A resource book released last year (unless it's an updated printing) will not be as accurate as one that came out only yesterday.

Jeff Foxworthy

You have to be relentless. With my first book, I got turned down by fourteen publishers—the first fourteen I went to.

I was actually on the road somewhere and was reading the newspaper one day and saw an article about Southern publishers. I was going down the list . . . yeah, they turned me down . . . they turned me down . . . Oh, here's one I haven't called! And I sent them a packet.

It was The Long Street Press and the editor called me up. He said, "I'd like to have a meeting with you. I think this will work. How does fifteen hundred dollars sound?"

Honestly, I was scared to answer. Because I didn't know if he was paying me or if he was asking me for fifteen hundred—which I didn't have! I was like, "Oh . . ." And he's like, "No, no, no! We'll pay you!" I said, "Oh yeah! That sounds great!"

I remember saying, "How many do you think we'll sell?"

He said, "I'll bet we'll sell about five thousand of them." That book sold about a million and a half copies. . . .

It's like anything in this business. You gotta be thick-skinned and do your research. I went to bookstores and tried to look for people who printed material similar to that. Then I went back, tried them, and got rejected by most of them. But I think that's a good piece of advice—to go find some type of publishing house that's doing something similar to what you want to do. Because at least they'll give it a look. If it's not up the alley of things they normally do, most places won't even read it.

FAQ 55 Any Advice for Someone Who Wants to Just Write for Other Comics?

I have been writing and performing stand-up for several years, but now, due to an eye condition (legally blind), I cannot travel. Any ideas how I can get my material to comedians? —D.

Many stand-up comics who have gone on to write for others have been discovered through their performances. As you undoubtedly know from your experience as a performer, an important part of the comedy business is networking. Not only do you get to know people within the industry, but they also get to know you and your material. If you've built a good reputation as a writer, the people you've worked with over the years will be aware of your talent.

These friendships and contacts made during your career can sometimes lead to writing jobs. For example, when Jay Leno took over *The Tonight Show*, he brought in some of his friends from the stand-up circuit as writers. Jerry Seinfeld and Larry David did the same for their hit sitcom, *Seinfeld*. These writers had worked clubs and associated with the performers for many years and knew the type of material that would be successful for that particular star's style and delivery.

Contacting comedians you've worked with would be a good starting point—if you honestly feel you can produce material that will work for them. Explain your goal of being a writer and offer to send them a sample. But be aware of two possible results:

1. Many comedians take pride in writing their own material. They may use suggestions or jokes given to them by other comics who've seen their performances, but are unwilling to pay for material if they have confidence in their own writing ability.

2. Know who your friends are. It would be a terrible experience to write a great set for someone, they reject the offer—and then you discover the comedian is performing your material and taking the credit.

In case you're not on a first-name basis with the next Leno or Seinfeld, you'll have to take a different route. In the larger entertainment cities, such as New York, Los Angeles, and Chicago, writers advertise their services in the trade papers. Comedians who find it difficult to write material could hire you to do it for them or as a collaborator. To do this correctly, you must take time to learn about the comedian's sense of humor and delivery so the material, can be tailored to fit her performance style. You'll also have to negotiate a fee, while keeping in mind a comedian searching the trade papers for a writer is probably not looking for someone to work on her next HBO special. Some writers charge per joke, routine, or set, while others use an hourly rate. As for exact prices, call some of the writers who are advertising their services, tell them you're looking for material, and ask what they charge. You can politely decline or say you need time to think it over, while learning what the going rate is in your market. If there are no comedy writers advertised, take a chance by setting your own price and see if there's any market at all.

Unless you already have credits as a writer, a good way to go about finding your price is to start low and build from there. This is similar to a comedian beginning his career as an open-mike act and looking to book his first paid job as an MC. In that position he's more inclined to accept low pay for the experience and résumé credit. If he's successful and becomes more in demand, his prices will increase—just like a comedian moving up to feature and headline status.

I've heard from writers who sell jokes from $5 to $50 each. A funny two- or three-minute bit can be worth more, and if the writer can produce a knock-out seven-minute set worthy of *The Tonight Show*, payment can be in the thousands of dollars. But as always, it depends *who* you are and *whom* you're selling it to.

When you write for other comedians, it's extremely important to do it in an honest way. In other words, don't sell the same jokes to different people. The comedy community is a tight one, and everyone will notice when two performers are doing the same jokes. After that, it won't be too difficult to find the source of the material and your reputation will only make you a writer to avoid.

This is the main reason why I advise comedians to be extremely careful about buying material from an unfamiliar source. In one of my workshops, an overanxious-for-stardom member didn't want to put in the effort to write his own act. He thought it was easy to bypass the work involved by purchasing his routine from someone contacted through a trade-paper advertisement. When he performed the material, most of us in the workshop had heard the jokes before and could call out the punch lines in advance. The only benefit he received by paying more than $50 for this set was an embarrassing lesson and the motivation to write his own material.

Another way to break into the writing business on a local level would be as a gag writer or humor consultant for public speakers. Contact area Toast-masters clubs and the National Speakers Association (NSA), and ask when they meet and how you can attend. Some of these organizations might charge a per-event fee or ask you to join as a member, but once you get involved it's a prime opportunity to network your ability as a comedy writer. The goal is to build credits and endorsements, then network your way to more and higher-paying jobs.

There are also writing groups formed by comics who are regular perform-ers at certain clubs or open mikes. They offer suggestions on material and critique various projects, while also keeping members aware of writing contests and job possibilities. I've seen this done with people who've taken my work-shops or met on the comedy scene and schedule regular meetings to work on routines, sketches, film scripts, and short stories. One group, The Comedy Kitchen (because, of course, their meetings are always in someone's kitchen) can even boast of a few members who've won contests and had scripts reviewed by Hollywood producers. Even if they haven't hit the grand prize and invited me to a movie premier, their individual list of writing credits continues to grow. Depending on your experience, the best way to find work as a comedy writer is through an agent. Many of the larger agencies have writing departments separate from agents who handle performers. If you've ever worked with anyone in the agency, contact that person and ask how to go about being represented as a writer. Whatever instructions or advice they give you concerning a submission or an interview, follow it closely and present yourself as a professional with samples and credits to prove it.

Without these contacts, it's a bit more difficult but still possible to obtain a writing agent through a great promotional package. The submission would include samples of your work, with quality being better than quantity.

If your primary skill is joke writing, send twenty of your best; five complete comedy bits lasting five to seven minutes in performance length will showcase your ability at exploring topics or telling stories. If you're interested in writing scripts for television sitcoms, pick the show for which you'd most like to write and submit your best effort to an agent (rarely will the actual show accept unsolicited manuscript submissions). Be sure to have a clear understanding of what the show is basically about and how each character has been portrayed in past episodes—including their manner of speaking, background, interests, employment, and anything else you've learned through being a loyal viewer. The Performing Arts sections in bookstores and libraries are full of how-to books about television scripts and presenting them in a professional manner. Learn the formatting techniques for dialogue, character movements, props, and even camera angles and include them in your finished script. The package should also include any credits (performing and writing) that prove you have experience in the comedy field. This is accomplished through a résumé and bio, along with any letters of recommendation, endorsement statements (giving credit to who said what and why), and mention of awards or achievements that will make your submission worth looking over. If you've done stand-up or had anyone perform your material, you might also include a video to show how it was delivered and the audience reaction.

As with any promotional package, have your contact information on each item in case the contents are separated for any reason. This would include a reliable phone number and e-mail address, along with a fax number and Web site if you have them. A business card will also give the package a more professional look.

After mailing the submission, use the earlier "staying in touch" methods until they've reviewed the package. Eventually, you should get an answer. In the meantime, don't stop writing. If it's really what you want to do, continue to improve and be ready for any opportunity that may come from all your hard work.

Jeff Cesario

I approached my career sort of like Herbie Hancock. He was a tremendous sideman for Miles Davis, and then he also had a great solo career. That's the way I always looked at it. I never looked at it like all I ever wanted to do is write and I always got

out of a situation writing for somebody else if I felt it was time. You know, I always had aspirations of my own. I think some guys are really happy just writing for other people. And that's great. They should definitely pursue that.

It was easy writing for Dennis (Miller) because our styles have some similarity anyway. And he's pretty easygoing in that arena. People always assume Dennis can be a bit of a handful, but that's one arena where he was a charm. He always told the writers, don't try to write a Dennis Miller joke. Just write jokes. He had a great eye for a good joke and he knew how to turn it into a Dennis Miller joke. You didn't have to worry about that.

I encourage young comics, if they're interested in writing or they want to break into writing, to try and write monologue jokes. To some extent, that pipeline has changed. There isn't a direct pipeline anymore to a Tonight Show or a Letterman. Those entities don't even use faxes anymore, I don't think. It used to be you could fax jokes and at some point, if you were getting enough on, they would hire you on some capacity. I don't think that's around anymore. But there are others, whether it's The Daily Show *or* The Man Show *or any of a variety of cable shows, there may be a place that a kid could submit some stuff to and see if they like it. Now there's different morning shows . . . Everybody is always kind of looking for something funny.*

Another way to do it is to go to the clubs. See the headliners—the locals and the nationals. If you're really interested more in writing than performing, then talk to the ones you like. Because that bond can work either way. If you like somebody and you like their style, it probably means you're going to have an affinity for writing for them. So don't hesitate to approach them. Walk right up and say, 'Hey listen, I'm a young comic and I'd love to know if you need any writing.' Because you know what, you never know. The person may not want any jokes for their act, but how many times is somebody gonna pop up hosting The Billboard Awards, The MTV Awards, The Country Music Awards, The Vibe Awards—there's twenty different awards shows now. Environments in which a good comedian with visibility is suddenly going to need ten writers and lots of material. That's when a Kevin James or a Ray Romano—or Ray Romano's head writer or Kevin James' head writer—may go, 'Okay, we just need volume.' And the guy goes, 'Well, this kid in Cleveland gave me two great jokes. Call him up and see if he wants to fax in twenty jokes.' And all of a sudden, you've worked your way in. So there's still ways to do it.

One of the ways I connected with Bob Costas—and I'm still a consultant on his HBO show—was years ago, he just saw my stand-up. And I do a lot of sports stuff. He really took a shine to it and called me. He had something that wasn't even on the air. It was just an awards banquet in New York somewhere and he was stuck on a couple of jokes. We kicked them around and came up with some funny stuff. From that, he said, "Listen, if we're ever in a position, let's work together." And I said I'd love to. Sure enough, with his HBO show, opportunity came around and I got hired. And my initial contact with him has got to be fifteen years ago, so you just never know when.

FAQ 56 Got Any Words for a Grand Finale?

Well, in the spirit of having a beginning, a middle, and an end, we can always say, "Thank you. Good night. You've been a great audience." Except there is a bit more . . .

There is no true "grand finale" when it comes to comedy. If you caught the essence of this book, you'll know comedy is an on-going, ever-evolving form of art, communication, and entertainment that has no end in sight. Laughter is a universal language. You can share it, enjoy it, or do both.

Being a comedian is an important occupation. It's a business of self-expression that not only brings joy to listeners, but also serves as a running commentary on where we are as individuals inhabiting the same world. People laughed a thousand years ago—and with any luck, they'll be laughing a thousand years from now. Comedians are reporters with commentaries based on imagination, creativity, and talent. When an audience laughs, the message has been delivered.

What's the best advice for anyone who wants to be a success in this noble profession? Being funny is the first one I can think of. A good business sense is another. But that's not the "grand finale." Only you can write that chapter.

Talent and experience count. As you travel down the road to becoming a successful comedian, you'll explore your talent and gain this experience. Hopefully, you'll take time—both on and off stage—to share it all with others who are only starting their journey.

But in the spirit of having "final words"—because this book has to end somewhere—I'll take the liberty of asking the final FAQ. As for my "grand finale"...

"Thank you. Good night. You've been a great audience."

FAQ 57 Help?

What's the best advice for anyone who wants to be a success in this noble profession? —Dave

George Carlin

If you're really in love with this idea, then you have to go do it. You have to give it a good, good long try. If you feel it very, very deeply and you feel like you can write a lot. . . .

You have to keep writing. You have to write down every note, every idea you get that seems potentially useful. When I was eighteen, I was in the air force and got a job on the radio station. I had a plan to get into radio first, then go to the stand-up stage and then try to use that to get into movies and TV. Just like everybody else does. You know? You use stand-up to get a TV or movie career, so nothing was different back in the 1950s. That's when I made these plans.

I was in radio in 1956. I was a young man, had just turned eighteen, and it was a good station. Number one in Shreveport. It sounds like a dinky town, but they had a nine-station market and it's a great radio town. So I worked there. And my first boss, Joe Monroe, who had a morning deejay show, said to me, "Write down every idea you get and put them away somewhere. Put them in folder. Put them somewhere, because the days will come when you don't have the ideas. Not every day, but you'll have a day or a week where you're trying to do something and you can't think of anything. You'll want to know that you'll have an arsenal. A storehouse."

So I began doing that then. Because I'm very left-brained and almost obsessive compulsive, I border on that, I had a need . . . have a need and always have, to keep files. And because the left brain wants to sort and be an indexer and a labeler, these files got names. These things got subdivisions. I now have two thousand computer files. If I could snap my fingers over my computer files, I could have five more HBO shows. In an instant. The problem with writing is it takes development and time at the writing stage, and then it takes development and time performing them so that you work out the kinks, and you learn the pieces and they get compact enough to do.

So my point is, always write down your ideas. Try to have a system for keeping them in order. And don't just have papers lying all over the house. Keep this shit in order. And from that, every time you see another one . . .

Let's say you write down ten things a day on little pieces of paper or in your hand recorder. Well, you might wait four or five days until you decide to put them in your files. You know, to get them out of the raw stage. Every time you look at that thing it goes through your head again. It runs the same neural path. When you think of the idea, the connection: "Oh, that's like that! It is a funny connection!" That's the beginning of a neural path.

As you write it down with your hand, the neural path gets a little more pronounced. As you look at it before you put it away, again there's another impression. When you put it in a little folder that you're carrying around, it stays there for a week and you decide to put your shit in files. Then you take it out and you look at it again. It makes the idea even deeper in your head. It's just a small idea, but the brain is a problem-solving, goal-seeking mechanism. The brain wants assignments. The subconscious mind is always working on making connections. Neural connections between different parts of an idea. It'll find things that are similar. It'll find places that these things naturally hook-up with. But they need to be seen often enough.

When you put it in a file . . . Let's say you're working with a computer. You put it in a file. It's about sports and it's a sports observation and you put it in a sports file. You wind up reading a few other things in that file. Those things are going in your head again. You take a minute and start to develop one of the lines into three or four lines. Or you think of something that goes with it. You know?

You must work on your ideas. And you must write, write, write, write, write. Have a lot of material. Have a lot of choices. If you find that you don't have that ability, if you're not a natural creator of comic material, I don't know how you can succeed unless you're a great ad-libber or a great improvisationist. That's a different story, but there aren't many of them.

Richard Jeni

If you're just starting out and the audience thinks you suck and the club owners think you suck and you think you suck, you're right on schedule. This is the type of job where it's all trial and error. There are a lot of books and classes and they're all helpful in their way, but really, the only way to become a comedian is through trial and error. By going on stage, bombing for ten minutes, then coming up with three jokes, you know? Bombing through another ten minutes and coming up with another joke. And you try a bunch of stuff, one thing works, and now you've got one. You try another bunch and one thing works, and now you have two. And then brick by brick you build up an act. It just takes [stage time].

You know, people say, 'Well, I tried comedy and I was no good at it.' And you say, 'Well, how many times did you do it?'

'Oh, I did it twice.'

Until you've been doing it for, like, three years, you really can't even judge whether you have a future in it or not.

For information about Dave Schwensen's comedy workshops and seminars, visit *www.thecomedybook.com*

CAST OF CHARACTERS
(Of course, all are stand-up comedians, except where noted)

JEFF ABRAHAM—Vice President, Jonas Public Relations, Santa Monica, California.

FLEX ALEXANDER—Star of the sitcom *One On One*. Appearances include *Showtime at the Apollo*.

HARRY ANDERSON—Comedian-magician. Star of the hit sitcoms *Night Court* and *Dave's World*.

DAVE ATTELL—Star of Comedy Central's *Insomniac*. Named one of the Top 100 Comedians of All Time by Comedy Central.

TED BARDY—Respected New York City acting coach. Owner, The Ted Bardy Studio.

LEWIS BLACK—America's Foremost Commentator on Everything. Awarded Best Male Stand-Up from *The American Comedy Awards*. Named one of the Top 100 Comedians of All Time by Comedy Central.

EDDIE BRILL—Comedian Talent Coordinator for *Late Show with David Letterman*. Winner of MAC Award three years in a row as Best Male Comedian in New York.

BRETT BUTLER—Star of the hit sitcom *Grace Under Fire*. Named one of the Top 100 Comedians of All Time by Comedy Central.

GEORGE CARLIN—Grammy and Emmy Awards winner, gold albums, television specials and appearances, recordings, film rolls and books are too numerous to mention—but here are a few: Over a dozen HBO Comedy Specials, hosted the very first *Saturday Night Live*, has a star on the Hollywood Walk of Fame, member of The Comedy Hall of Fame, and Life Time Achievement Award from The American Comedy Awards. One of the most influential comedians ever to walk on a stage. Period.

JEFF CESARIO—Winner of two Emmy Awards and six Cable Ace Awards. Writer and producer for *The Larry Sanders Show* and *Dennis Miller Live*. Award-winning stand-up specials and appearances on *The Tonight Show with Jay Leno* and *Late Show with David Letterman*.

MARGARET CHO—American Comedy Awards "Female Stand-Up of the Year." Writer-star of off-Broadway and film hits, *I'm The One That I Want* and *Notorious C.H.O.* Television special, *Revolution*.

ELLEN CLEGHORNE—Emmy Award–winning cast member of *Saturday Night Live*. Star of the sitcom, *Cleghorne*, and the one-woman show, *Behind Funny*. Films include *Armageddon*, *Little Nicky*, and *Coyote Ugly*.

BOBBY COLLINS—Star of his own Showtime Special and host of *VH-1's Stand-Up Spotlight*. Toured with Cher, Juilo Iglesias, and Dolly Parton.

MARK CURRY—Star of the hit sitcom *Hangin' with Mr. Cooper* and host of *It's Showtime at the Apollo*. Appearances include *The Tonight Show with Jay Leno*, *Oprah*, *The Drew Carey Show*, *Celebrity Mole*, and host of BET's *Coming to the Stage* and ABC's *Bachelor Pad*.

ROBERT DUBAC—Writer, director, and star, (playing numerous characters), of the hit one-man shows, *The Male Intellect: An Oxymoron?, Inside The Male Intellect,* and *Piss and Moan.*

EARTHQUAKE—Star of his own Comedy Central special, the *Crown Royal Comedy Soul Fest,* and a One Hour Platinum Series comedy special.

BILL ENGVALL—American Comedy Awards "Male Stand-Up of the Year." Star of "The Blue Collar Tour" and movie and television show of the same name.

MIKE EPPS—Star of *Def Comedy Jam* and numerous feature films including *Next Friday, Friday After Next, The Fighting Temptations,* and *The Honeymooners.*

CHARLES FLEISCHER—Numerous film and television roles including the voice of Roger Rabbit in the hit Disney film, *Who Framed Roger Rabbit."* A master at on-stage comedy ad-lib.

JEFF FOXWORTHY—The largest-selling comedy-recording artist in history, multiple Grammy Award–nominee and best selling author of eleven books. Named one of the Top 100 Comedians of All Time by Comedy Central.

GREG GIRALDO—*Late Show with David Letterman, Late Night with Conan O'Brien, Tough Crowd with Colin Quinn,* and his own Comedy Central special.

BOBCAT GOLDTHWAIT—Film and television director and writer. Star of the *Police Academy* movies. Named one of the Top 100 Comedians of All Time by Comedy Central.

BRIAN HEFFRON—President, Heffron Talent International and The Comedy Zones, Charlotte, North Carolina.

MARYELLEN HOOPER—Best Female Stand-Up Comic from *The American Comedy Awards.* Appearances include *The Tonight Show with Jay Leno* and her own *Lounge Lizards* special on Comedy Central.

DOM IRRERA—Cable Ace Award winner for HBO's *One Night Stand* and as host for Showtime's *Full Frontal Comedy*. Named one of the Top 100 Comedians of All Time by Comedy Central and won the Herald Award for artistic excellence at the Edinburgh Fringe Comedy Festival in the U.K.

RICHARD JENI—Awards for HBO and Showtime comedy specials and Best Male Stand-Up from *The American Comedy Awards*. Named one of the Top 100 Comedians of All Time by Comedy Central.

DAVE JUSKOW—New York City–based writer and filmmaker.

JANN KARAM—*The Tonight Show with Johnny Carson, Late Show with David Letterman,* and *Seinfeld*. Star of the one-woman show, *Reclining Nude on La Cienega*.

BARRY KATZ—New Wave Entertainment. Executive Producer of NBC's *Last Comic Standing*.

JONATHAN KATZ—a.k.a. Dr. Katz, Professional Therapist. Emmy Award–winning comedian.

DEBBIE KELLER—Owner of Personal Publicity, Tempe, Arizona.

LISA LAMPANELLI—Comedy's Lovable Queen of Mean from BET, Comedy Central, and heard on *The Howard Stern Show*.

ROCKY LAPORTE—Television appearances include *The Tonight Show with Jay Leno, Cheers,* and *Caroline's Comedy Hour*.

WENDY LIEBMAN—Best Female Stand-Up from *The American Comedy Awards*. Appearances include *Late Show with David Letterman, The Tonight Show with Johnny Carson, The Tonight Show with Jay Leno,* television specials on HBO and Comedy Central.

BRAD LOWERY—Nominated "Best College Comedian" four years in a row. Appearances include *Showtime at the Apollo* and *Def Comedy Jam*.

KATHLEEN MADIGAN—Best Female Stand-Up from *The American Comedy Awards*. Appearances include her HBO and Comedy Central Specials, *Late Show with David Letterman, The Tonight Show with Jay Leno,* and *Last Comic Standing*.

KATE MAGILL—College Agent. Owner of Sophie K. Entertainment, New York City.

AL MARTIN—Owner of numerous New York City comedy clubs including The Improv and The New York Comedy Club.

JACKIE "THE JOKE MAN" MARTLING—Former Head Writer for *The Howard Stern Show*.

CHRIS MURPHY—New York City Comedy Coach. Appearances include *An Evening At The Improv* and *Caroline's Comedy Hour*.

FLIP ORLEY—Comedian-hypnotist. Appearances include *The Today Show* and *Entertainment Tonight*. Also works on clinical side of hypnosis with seminars and workshops on stress, weight loss, and other topics.

GREG PROOPS—A regular on the long-running British television show *Whose Line Is It Anyway?* and frequent appearances on the U.S. version. Stars in *Drew Carey's Green Screen Show*.

BRIAN REGAN—Winner of Best Club Comedian at the American Comedy Awards. Appearances include *Late Show with David Letterman, The Tonight Show with Johnny Carson, Late Night with Conan O'Brien,* and his own specials on Comedy Central and Showtime.

DENNIS REGAN—*Late Show with David Letterman* and *The Tonight Show with Jay Leno*. Television writer for *The King of Queens*.

RAY ROMANO—Emmy Award–winning star of the hit sitcom, *Everybody Loves Raymond*. Named one of the Top 100 Comedians of All Time by Comedy Central.

BOBBY SLAYTON—The Pit Bull of Comedy. Best Male Stand-Up by *The American Comedy Awards*. Named one of the Top 100 Comedians of All Time by Comedy Central.

BRUCE SMITH—Founder and partner, Omnipop, Inc. Talent Agency, Los Angeles and New York.

CHRISTOPHER TITUS—Star of the innovative sitcom *Titus* and his own one-man show, *Norman Rockwell Is Bleeding*. Appearances include *The Tonight Show with Jay Leno* and *Politically Incorrect*. Films include *Killer Klowns from Outer Space*.

GEORGE WALLACE—Best Male Stand-Up from *The American Comedy Awards* and named one of the Top 100 Comedians of All Time by Comedy Central.

PAT WILSON—Owner, Comedy West Agency and Odyssey Management, Seattle, Washington.

WEIRD AL YANKOVIC—Multiple Grammy Award–winner for song parodies including Best Comedy Album, Best Comedy Recording, and Best Concept Video.

INDEX

Books from Allworth Press

Allworth Press is an imprint of Allworth Communications, Inc. Selected titles are listed below.

Writing Television Comedy
by Jerry Rannow (paperback, 6 × 9, 224 pages, $14.95)

Promoting Your Acting Career: A Step-by-Step Guide to Opening the Right Doors, Second Edition
by Glenn Alterman (paperback, 6 × 9, 240 pages, $19.95)

Career Solutions for Creative People: How to Balance Artistic Goals with Career Security
by Dr. Ronda Ormont (paperback, 6 × 9, 320 pages, $19.95)

Improv for Actors
by Dan Diggles (paperback, 6 × 9, 224 pages, $19.95)

The Art of Auditioning: Techniques for Television
by Rob Decina (paperback, 6 × 9, 288 pages, $19.95)

Creating Your Own Monologue
by Glenn Alterman (paperback, 6 × 9, 208 pages, $14.95)

Surviving Hollywood: Your Ticket to Success
by Jerry Rannow (paperback, 6 × 9, 224 pages, $16.95)

Making It on Broadway: Actors' Tales of Climbing to the Top
by David Wienir and Jodie Langel (paperback, 6 × 9, 288 pages, $19.95)

Creative Careers in Hollywood
by Laurie Scheer (paperback, 6 × 9, 240 pages, $19.95)

Booking and Tour Management for the Performing Arts, Third Edition
by Rena Shagan (paperback, 6 × 9, 288 pages, $19.95)

The Health and Safety Guide for Film, TV and Theater
by Monona Rossol (paperback, 6 × 9, 256 pages, $19.95)

Please write to request our free catalog. To order by credit card, call 1-800-491-2808 or send a check or money order to Allworth Press, 10 East 23rd Street, Suite 510, New York, NY 10010. Include $5 for shipping and handling for the first book ordered and $1 for each additional book. Ten dollars plus $1 for each additional book if ordering from Canada. New York State residents must add sales tax.

To see our complete catalog on the World Wide Web, or to order online, you can find us at **www.allworth.com.**